Dan T. Alighieri is the author of the unbelievably popular Robert Blandon series. Only the Bible has sold more copies, and that hardly has any chase scenes. He ploughs many of his profits into the Dan T. Alighieri Foundation, which raises awareness of conspiracy theories in children of developing countries.

He has been awarded the prestigious 'Best Use of Italics' award by *Airport Thriller Review* for the last ten years running.

He has chosen to release this book at exactly 6:29am on May 14th 2013, i.e. 5/14/13. A meaningless sequence of numbers, you might think. But run them backwards and you get 3.1415926, or pi to seven places. And then you remember you're in your living room. One of the *seven places* you like to eat pie.

Coincidence?

*There's no such thing, sheeple.*

# DAN'S INFERNO

## Dan T. Alighieri

MICHAEL O'MARA BOOKS LIMITED

First published in Great Britain in 2013 by
Michael O'Mara Books Limited
9 Lion Yard
Tremadoc Road
London SW4 7NQ

A CIP catalogue record for this book is available from the British Library.

Papers used by Michael O'Mara Books Limited are natural, recyclable
products made from wood grown in sustainable forests. The manufacturing
processes conform to the environmental regulations of the country of origin.

ISBN: 978-1-78243-144-2 in paperback print format
ISBN: 978-1-78243-160-2 in ebook format

2 3 4 5 6 7 8 9 10

Note: The character of Robert Blandon is breathtakingly original to the
author and should not be confused with any similar sounding characters now
known or hereinafter invented.

Designed and typeset by Design23

Printed and bound by CPI Group (UK) Ltd, Croydon, CR0 4YY

www.mombooks.com

**Fact:**

All artwork, literature, bits of science and locations mentioned in this novel are real. You, on the other hand, live in a flotation tank and have all your experiences injected directly into your brain by the Freemasons.

The 'Conspiratorium' is a private organization with offices in seventy countries. I have changed their name so they don't assassinate me near a grassy knoll in Dallas. Believe me, they have form.

## Acknowledgements

Thanks to everyone on the Irate Paranoid Nutjob forum and the Wishy Washy Institute for New Age Studies in California for their help with my extensive research for this work of art. No thanks to the Illuminati for making my laptop crash during Chapter 36 so I had to write it again. Don't pretend it wasn't you, guys. I know it was.

## Prologue

*I have become the shade.*

By that I don't mean that I've become the obscure DC Comics villain or the minor character from one of the Sonic the Hedgehog games. I mean I've become one of the bodiless souls from Dante's *Inferno*.

In the highly likely event you haven't read it, 'Inferno' is the name given to the first part of Dante Alighieri's epic poem *The Divine Comedy*. It features some pretty cool descriptions of sinners being punished in hell. Judas Iscariot gets the worst treatment, though it was written before TV talent show judges existed.

*I have become the shade.*

Sorry, I know I've already said that. I just think it will make this section a bit more exciting if I keep repeating it.

*I have become the shade.*

See?

*Through the city I pass.*

I run past the Uffizi, one of the most famous art galleries in the world. It was built in 1560 as offices for local magistrates, and opened to the public in 1765. It houses famous works by artists such as Giotto, Botticelli, Michelangelo and Raphael.

I look to the north, and see the Apennine Mountains, a mountain range extending 1200km (750mi). The highest peak is Corno Grande, which is 2912m (9554ft).

I pass the Museo del Bargello, a former army barracks and prison, it is now home to masterpieces by Michelangelo, Donatello, Vincenzo Gemito and Robert Mapplethorpe [*citation needed*].

*I have become the shade.*

This is actually quite educational, isn't it? There you were, casually reading an action-packed prologue, and before you knew it, you'd learnt about the Uffizi gallery, the Apennine Mountains and the Museo del Bargello. If any of that stuff ever comes up in a pub quiz or on *Who Wants to be a Millionaire?* you'll be sorted.

*I have become the shade.*

I wrench aside the iron gate at the foot of the Badia Fiorentina and tumble inside. I force myself up the marble steps into the cold air and stare down at the city with my green eyes and short blonde hair.

*I take the 9mm Glock 17 Gen 4 from my pocket.*

*I do this to keep the secret.*

*It is my gift to mankind.*

*It is my duty.*

*It is my inferno.*

*I just said the title.*

I hope you've enjoyed this first person prologue. The text switches to third person now. You're not meant to imagine me standing on top of the tower reading out the rest of the book, though. It's just something thriller writers do. I don't know why. They probably teach it in thriller college, right after the modules on ending chapters with cliff-hangers and incorporating random flames into the cover design.

Sorry, I'm rambling now. I really wanted a punchy ending for this bit, too. The last thing I want is for all you lot in the airport bookshop to put this back on the shelf and spend your entire flight listening to 'Gangnam Style' on repeat instead.

Honestly, this will be worth reading. There will be loads of puzzles and tunnels and at the end you'll learn the hidden truth that the world has been keeping secret from you all your life.

Where was I? Oh yeah.

*I have become the shade.*
*This is my gift.*
*This is my destiny.*
*This is my inferno.*
*I pull the trigger.*

# Chapter 1

*What the hell?* thought Blandon.

He was looking out across a river of blood at a pile of corpses that were writhing in unspeakable pain, clawing and gnashing at each other. They looked over at him with pleading eyes, their loud shrieks of agony echoing across the churning blood.

'Are you all right?' asked Blandon. 'Do you need me to fetch anyone?'

The corpses only screamed louder in reply.

The air around him was thick with the oppressive stench of decay, death and desperation. It smelt like someone had shit their pants.

'Where am I?' cried Blandon. 'What do you want?'

The bodies multiplied, writhing around and screaming. There were hundreds of them, thousands, millions.

'Oh God!' shouted Blandon. He'd had a phobia of mounds of writhing, smelly bodies ever since he'd visited a rock festival as a student.

Blandon woke up.

That's right, we started with a dream sequence. Deal with it.

# Chapter 2

*What the hell?* thought Blandon.

He was in a bed in a bright room. The air was heavy with the smell of hospital medicine and the sound of hospital machines.

*Where am I?* he wondered.

He turned to the right and saw an IV drip sticking out

of his arm.

*I'm in a hospital,* he thought. *What the hell?*

Blandon's head stung with impossible pain. He lifted his hand to the back of his thick brown mullet and stuck his finger into a large hole. It poked right through to his skull.

*A bullet hole,* he thought. *I've been shot.*

*Why have I been shot?*

*Who would want to shoot me?*

*I'm one of the best-loved people in the world.*

Blandon stared out of the window at the dark night and tried to piece together what had happened. He'd been invited to Florence to deliver a lecture to thousands of eager puzzleology students at the university. He was the world's greatest puzzleologist and had been described as 'the cleverest person in the world' by *Brainy Tweed-Clad Academic Monthly*.

He'd been looking forward to delivering his lecture, and was going to cover really hard topics like cryptic crosswords, palindromes and expert-level Tetris. But he'd never even reached the lecture hall.

*Why?*

Blandon thought back to earlier in the day. He'd flown into Florence airport in a Falcon 2000EX corporate jet, which had a height of 7.06 metres and a length of 20.23 metres. He'd listened to the unmistakable sound of the Pratt and Whitney R-2800 engines as he'd studied his lecture notes.

The jet had taxied to a private terminal and Blandon had been greeted by a sleek limousine and climbed into the luxurious interior. It had been just like any other foreign visit for an academic. *What had gone wrong?*

They'd driven into the centre of Florence, where he'd been scheduled to meet Professor Companion, the head of the Florence University Puzzleology Faculty. And then... what?

What had happened?

Blandon looked at his reflection in the hospital window. He was handsome and charming, in a way that reminded everyone of Harrison Ford. Or Tom Hanks, if Harrison Ford doesn't want to do it.

He was wearing his regular tweed jacket, black turtleneck sweater, khaki trousers and loafers. It was what all the cleverest professors and thriller authors wore.

Blandon heard footsteps in the corridor.

*At last,* he thought. *Someone's going to tell me what's going on.*

The door swung open and an angry Italian policeman stepped inside.

*What the hell?* thought Blandon.

## Chapter 3

'What happened last night?' asked Blandon.

'I was hoping you might be able to tell me,' said the policeman. He had wide angry nostrils, like those of an enraged bull. His angry hair was slicked back like that of an annoyed otter. His small angry eyes were like those of a disgruntled ferret. 'Allow me to introduce myself. I'm Inspector Fascist of the Florence Police Force.'

'I'm Robert Blandon,' said Robert Blandon.

'Like I don't already know,' spat Fascist. 'You're the most famous puzzleologist in the world. We've had to spend all night turning away starstruck fans who are desperate to get their copies of *Crosswords and the Sacred Feminine* signed.'

Blandon chuckled to himself. His last book, which had proved that the descendants of Christ were still alive and setting the clues for cryptic crosswords in broadsheet newspapers, had caused quite a stir. He hadn't meant it to. He was simply stating the facts. Not boring facts based on evidence and research like those other stuffy professors used, but more exciting ones that he thought up himself.

'So why don't you take me through what you do remember?' sneered Fascist, dripping sarcasm all over the hospital floor. 'If it's not too much trouble, that is.'

'I was on my way to meet Professor Companion,' said Blandon. He trawled his sharp mind for more details, but all he dredged up were the writhing bodies from his dream. 'That's all I got.'

'How very convenient,' asserted Fascist angrily.

'What do you mean?' asked Blandon, his heart pumping faster.

'Professor Companion is dead,' said Fascist. 'And you were the last person to meet him.'

'What the hell?' asked Blandon.

## Chapter Pi

'Dead?' asked Blandon. 'But he can't be. I spoke to him just yesterday.'

Blandon couldn't believe Professor Companion was dead. He'd been in charge of one of the most renowned puzzleology faculties in Europe. He'd been a popular figure at home and abroad.

And now he was dead.

Dead?

Dead.

*Dead.*

*But how?*

'But how?' asked Blandon.

Fascist sighed and tossed a gory Polaroid at Blandon. At first Blandon thought he was looking at a slaughterhouse bin, but as he peered closer he saw the naked form of an old dead man. He had been shot in the heart then his torso had been slit from groin to neck. The dead old man was holding the flaps of skin back to reveal his own sticky entrails.

'Bring anything back?' asked Fascist.

'Nothing,' said Blandon.

*Except perhaps my lunch*, he chuckled to himself.

'Look at the words on the floor,' said Fascist.

Blandon peered at the photo. He could just about make out some words scrawled in blood on the stone piazza next to the body.

'As he was dying from his gunshot wound, Companion slit his own stomach open and used his blood to write these words on the ground. Do they mean anything to you?'

Blandon peered at the words. They read:

My first is in peaceable but not in place
My second is in mortal but not in marmot
My third is in irrigate but not in tiger
My fourth is in crooner but not in coercer
My fifth is in supersede but not in purse
My sixth is in vegetation but not in negative
My seventh is in nought but not in ought

'What does it mean?' asked Fascist.

'I need time,' said Blandon. 'This is a really hard puzzle.'

'Well you'd better get a move on,' said Fascist. 'Because here's what I'm thinking. You met up with the professor last night and got into some argument about puzzles or symbols or some such intellectual nonsense. Things turned ugly. He shot you in the head and you got revenge by slitting him open and pulling his entrails out.'

'You've got it all wrong,' pleaded Blandon, his head quite literally spinning around.

Blandon tried again to remember but nothing came back to him.

*Nothing.*


## Chapter 4

'What's going on in here?' purred a woman's voice. 'I don't remember giving anyone permission to see my patient.'

A woman wearing blue scrubs strode in. She had long blonde hair and a strong, delicate gait like a medal-winning athlete who has retired to become a florist. Although she was only in her early twenties, Blandon could tell from her profound brown eyes that she'd experienced an unusual amount of pain for someone her age. He could tell from the small beauty spot above her lips that she had a keen, inquisitive mind. And he could tell from her left earlobe that she had a warm heart beneath her cold exterior.

'I need to talk to Mr Blandon,' said Fascist. 'It's a matter of vital importance.'

'It will have to wait,' said the doctor. 'Mr Blandon will be able to answer your questions when he's recovered.'

Fascist snorted like an angry gazelle as the lady doctor ushered him out of the room.

'Thanks,' said Blandon. 'I really appreciate you helping me out like this, doctor.'

'I'm not a doctor,' said the woman. She ripped her blue scrubs off to reveal a tweed jacket, black turtleneck sweater, khaki pants and loafers. 'I'm a puzzleologist.'

'What the hell?' asked Blandon.

## Chapter 5

On the street outside the hospital, a lithe woman with fierce animal determination in her eyes leapt from her BMW S1000RR bike, which had a 999cc inline-4 engine, had a top speed of 305 km/h (190 mph) and could do 0-100 km/h in 3.1 seconds.

The woman's sharp, unforgiving green eyes smouldered with animal conviction. She ran a hand through her cropped blonde hair and smoothed down her leather riding suit.

She strode towards the hospital with human purpose. Tonight she'd made a mistake.

Now she was going to put it right.

She was going to aim her 9mm Glock 17 Gen 4 at Robert Blandon's mullety head once again.

*And this time he wouldn't survive.*

## Chapter 6

'Allow me to introduce myself,' said the woman. 'I'm Florence. Florence Companion.'

Of course, thought Blandon. He'd recognized those deep profound eyes. They were the eyes of Professor Companion. *Her father.*

'I'm Robert Blandon,' said Blandon. 'I'm a puzzleologist too.'

'I know,' said Florence. 'We studied your book *Su Doku and the New World Order* in university. It's the best thing I've ever read.'

Blandon chuckled to himself. The establishment had absolutely shat itself when he'd published that two decades ago. Now they were teaching it to college kids.

*All great truths begin as blasphemies*, thought Blandon. No matter how often he tried to explain this to mankind, it didn't seem to sink in.

'I'm sorry for your loss,' said Blandon.

'Yes,' said Florence, looking down at the floor. Suddenly her confident bluster was replaced by the trembling sigh of a lost little girl. 'Dead... Dad... Dad... Dead. It still doesn't seem real.'

Florence's confident tone reappeared. 'But never mind about all that. We need to get you out of here.'

'Out of here?' protested Blandon. He pointed to his bleeding head. 'What about this?'

'It will be the least of your worries if we don't leave right now,' yapped Florence. She held up a copy of the Polaroid Inspector Fascist had been carrying and pointed to the words scrawled on the floor. 'Haven't you worked this out yet?'

Blandon willed the words to make sense. But it was no use. The puzzle was too hard.

'Don't you see?' asked Florence. '"Blandon" is the answer to the puzzle. *The only answer*. You can bet Fascist has got the police puzzleology department working on this right now. And as soon as they work it out, you'll be transferred straight from the hospital to the prison.'

'The prison?' spluttered Blandon. 'They'd think I murdered your father? But what proof would they have?'

'Oh please,' snorted Florence. 'You are not in your

precious America now. As soon as they realize that my dad named you in the puzzle, they'll have all the proof they need to lock you up and throw away the key.'

Blandon leapt up from the hospital bed and yanked the IV drip out of his arm. 'So what do we do?'

Florence darted over to the window and slid it open. 'We jump out of here,' she said.

## Chapter 7

Inspector Fascist rushed back down the hospital corridor like a peeved ostrich. The puzzleology department had finally come back to him, and it was good news. Not good news for the mullet-headed American, of course, but good news for him.

The answer to the puzzle the dying professor had scrawled was 'Blandon'. That was enough to convict him of murder in any Italian court. But it would never get that far. Professor Companion had been one of the most popular academics in the country. As soon he tipped off the papers that Blandon was the only suspect, an angry mob would descend on the station and tear him to pieces.

*And Fascist would look the other way.*

Why should he care? All he had to do was drag Blandon out of the hospital bed and down to the station. Then his job would be done. And this time he wouldn't listen to any meddling doctors.

Fascist kicked the door aside angrily.

The bed was empty.

*Blandon was gone.*

A trail of blood led from the bed to the open window.

Blue nurse's scrubs had been discarded on the floor.

Fascist snorted angry air out of his incensed nostrils.

*Tricked.*

He'd been tricked by the murderous professor and a puzzleology fan posing as a doctor.

He was sick and tired of Americans stomping onto his patch, killing people and assuming they could get away with it.

Well, this time he wasn't going to stand for it. He took his Beretta 93R single action automatic pistol out of his pocket and rushed for the door.

## Chapter 8

Florence grabbed Blandon and pulled him into a doorway as the police car sped past. Blandon imagined Inspector Fascist inside it, scowling like an angry lion that could drive.

Blandon took his cell phone out of his pocket but Florence snatched it out of his hands.

'Is there anyone you need to call on this? A wife? Children?' Florence asked.

Blandon loved his life as an independent, carefree bachelor and had never wanted to get tied down to one woman. He'd had a lot of offers, sure. With his massive lecturer's salary, the huge royalties that poured in from his academic publications, and his Indiana Jones (or failing that, Forrest Gump) good looks, he was desirable to hot, clever women.

He'd had a string of romances with attractive, virtually identical professional women. There had been Rome Sidekick, Paris Tourguide and Washington Loveinterest. They'd all made love to him, often as a reward for defeating villains, which was actually quite sexist when you thought about it. But he'd never kept in touch with any of them.

*It just wasn't his way.*

'No,' asserted Blandon powerfully. 'There's no one like that.'

Florence grabbed his phone and tossed it into the River Arno, which is 241km (150mi) long, originates in the Apennine Mountains and flows through Florence, Empoli and Pisa on its way to the Ligurian Sea.

'What the hell?' asked Blandon.

'I'm sorry,' said Florence. 'But that's the first thing they'll check when they're tracing you. Any schoolboy with a laptop could find you through that thing these days.'

*Great*, thought Blandon. *There goes my chance of calling for help.* But who could he trust anyway? If experience had taught him anything, it was that generic beautiful female companions were the only people he could trust.

'Okay,' said Blandon. 'So how do we find the killer? Do you think it might be someone else called Blandon?'

'That's what I thought at first,' said Florence. 'Then I saw this.'

Florence pointed at the bottom of the Polaroid. It turned out that her dying dad had daubed the words 'Mega hell icon' onto the saggy white skin of his calf.

'What the hell?' asked Blandon.

'After my father was shot then slit his own stomach open, pulled the entrails out and scrawled the riddle on the floor, he wrote these words on his leg,' said Florence.

'But what do they mean?' spluttered Blandon.

He rubbed his severe head wound. Usually a riddle like this would be no problem at all for him, but the gaping hole in his head was impairing his puzzle ability.

*Just when he needed it most of all.*

'I can tell you're trying to solve the puzzle,' said Florence. 'But there's no need. I've already done it. He wants us to go to a large painting of hell. Namely, Fra Angelico's "The Last Judgment" in San Marco church.'

*Of course*, thought Blandon.

*Mega hell icon.*

*Large painting of hell.*

*Why hadn't he seen this?*

'The Last Judgment' was a painting by Renaissance artist Fra Angelico. It showed Christ sitting in judgment, with heaven on the right side and hell on the left side. The *sinistra* side.

*It's a secret message from Professor Companion*, thought Blandon. *He's sending us to the San Marco church.*

*But why?*

Maybe there was a clue to the professor's real killer there.

Maybe he'd sent someone there to help them.

Either way, it was where they needed to go.

'Quick!' shouted Blandon. 'We need to get to the church!'


## Chapter 9

The assassin scooped some of the blood from the hospital floor and lifted it to her tongue.

It was over ten minutes old.

It looked as though the mullet-headed professor had escaped her again.

But did it really matter?

Maybe having that foolish puzzleologist on the run would help distract the police from the real killer.

*Which was her.*

Anyway, she'd take care of Blandon when the time came.
*By killing him.*

In the meantime, the Pathfinder had given her work to do.

*Some more killings.*

She jumped out of the window, landed on her bike and tore away down the street.

## Chapter 10

Florence and Blandon ran across the Ponte Vecchio, the bridge that crosses the Arno at its narrowest point. The original bridge dated back to Roman times, but the current structure dates back to the fourteenth century, and is still lined with shops.

Blandon chuckled to himself. The American tourists who bought jewellery and souvenirs from these shops would have no idea they were originally occupied by the town butchers, who used to toss rotten meat into the river. Or that a secret passageway called the Vasari Corridor ran across the bridge.

'There's a secret passageway crossing this bridge called the Vasari Corridor,' Blandon foreshadowed.

'I've always wanted to visit it,' said Florence, with ironic overtones that won't become apparent until Chapter 58. 'I expect I'll have a really nice time when I finally get round to it.'

Blandon's impressive mind fluttered back to the anagrams module he'd taught on the puzzleology course back at Harvard.

He'd turned away from the ocean of eager faces and

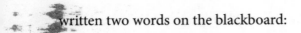written two words on the blackboard:

AXL ROSE

A gasp shook the classroom. His students had been expecting to learn about fusty old dodderers like Isaac Newton and William Shakespeare. And yet their tweed-clad professor was teaching them about rock and roll.

*Were they losing their minds?*

'What do you think when you see this name?' asked Blandon.

'*Appetite for Destruction,*' shouted a long-legged jock from the back of the class. He raised his hand and made the sign of the horns by extending his index finger and little finger while holding his two other fingers down with his thumb.

Blandon chuckled to himself. He knew that before this symbol was adopted by the heavy metal community, it was used in primitive cultures to ward off evil. In fact, most of the symbology of heavy metal culture, such as growing your hair long, screaming in a silly high voice and pissing in a plastic bottle and lobbing it at the stage, had exactly the same origin.

But that wasn't a lesson for today.

*One step at a time.*

'You know what I think of?' asked Blandon.

He turned back to the blackboard and wrote the words:

ORAL SEX

This time the gasps were so loud they made the ancient foundations of the college, which was founded in 1636, shudder.

'Woah,' shouted the long-legged jock. 'Are you trying to

tell us something, sir?'

Frat boys coughed out puerile giggles.

'I'm trying to tell you that I think of "Oral sex" because it's an anagram of "Axl Rose", said Blandon. 'An anagram is the name given when we rearrange the letters of a word or phrase to create a new one.'

The students began to frantically scribble notes down in their textbooks.

'Pay attention,' said Blandon. 'Because some of these will be coming up in your exam.'

He scribbled down more anagrams on the board, each one drawing fresh gasps.

JUSTIN TIMBERLAKE = I'M A JERK, BUT LISTEN

CLINT EASTWOOD = OLD WEST ACTION

VIN DIESEL = I END LIVES

Blandon had loved watching the expressions of confusion, disbelief and finally joy on the faces of the students as they stared at the words. But why was he remembering this now?

He needed to get to the Mega hell icon – why was his mind turning to anagrams?

Blandon stopped in his tracks.

He thanked his clever brain for helping him once again.

Mega hell icon *was* an anagram.

## Chapter 11

'Stop!' shouted Blandon. 'We're going the wrong way!'

'Come on!' yelled Florence. 'We need to get to the San Marco church before Inspector Fascist. He'll speed over there as soon as his puzzleology team work out what the message means.'

Blandon gasped for breath. Even though he was one of the strongest and most agile professors in the whole of Harvard, running with a serious head wound was taking its toll.

'We shouldn't be going to the San Marco church,' he spluttered. 'We should be going to the Palazzo Vecchio.'

'The Palazzo Vecchio?' spluttered Florence back. 'But there's no large painting of hell there.'

'No,' said Blandon. 'But there is a replica of Michelangelo's *David*. Don't you see? "Mega hell icon" doesn't refer to a large painting of hell. It's an anagram of "Michelangelo".'

*Of course*, thought Florence. *She looked down at the ground and thick tears formed in her profound eyes.*

*Mega hell icon.*

*Michelangelo.*

*Why hadn't she worked it out?*

All her life her father had wanted her to become a great puzzleologist. Every morning he'd made her complete ten cryptic crosswords and twelve Su Dokus before she was allowed to eat or drink.

He'd been relying on her to solve the puzzle, and she'd let him down.

'You haven't let anyone down,' soothed Blandon generously. 'That was a really hard puzzle. Even I didn't spot it at first.'

'I just thought about how disappointed he would be,' said

Florence. 'My father wanted me to be a great puzzleologist one day. Like you.'

Blandon chuckled to himself. 'Who knows? You might be, one day. But you're doing just fine for now, kid.'

He wiped a tear from the side of her gentle eye.

'Now let's get to that *David* sculpture,' he urged.


## Chapter 12

Inspector Fascist slammed open the door to the San Marco church and stormed angrily in.

His blood boiled as he rampaged down the aisle, holding his handgun in front of him. For once his puzzleology department had given him results he could use. As soon as they'd worked out that 'Mega hell icon' referred to the large painting in the San Marco church, he'd raced across the ancient city in his Fiat Freemont with front wheel drive, automatic six speed gearbox and 6034 cubic cm engine.

Blandon would surely still be here.

He couldn't have missed him.

'Come out, Mr Blandon,' hissed Fascist. 'You have nothing to fear from me. I simply want to help.'

*And maybe pop a few more bullets into your brain and pretend you died in the struggle to escape*, smiled Fascist to himself.

Fascist stalked up to the painting at the front of the church and shone his flashlight on it.

There was no one there.

*That clever professor with his fancy American ways had outsmarted him.*

Fascist let out a howl of rage and fired a round of bullets into the painting.

## Chapter 13

Blandon rushed across the Piazza della Signoria towards the Palazzo Vecchio, the old town hall. Built between 1298 and 1314 for the Florentine government, it still houses the mayor's office today and is crowned by the famous 94m (308ft) Torre di Arnolfo.

In front of the building was the replica of Michelangelo's *David*. Blandon chuckled as he thought of all the American tourists who pointed their cameras at the replica, assuming it was the original.

The sculpture itself was moved to the Accademia Gallery in 1873, and this replica was placed in the original location.

Professor Companion had sent them here, via a message only brilliant puzzleologists would find.

*But why had he sent them here?*

There was no one to help them.

There was no clue about his killer scrawled anywhere.

Blandon ran his hands through his mullet. Blood was still flowing freely down the back of his head. Surely he hadn't used up all that clever puzzle-solving energy just to arrive at a dead end.

Florence stroked her chin and sifted through her reasonably intelligent mind. Suddenly, her profound eyes blazed with understanding.

'This sculpture is called David!' she exclaimed. 'Maybe someone called David killed him.'

Blandon thought about this. It made a hell of a lot of sense, but who did they both know called David?

The only person he could think of was the respected historian David Icke. Blandon had attended one of his lectures in London, and had been shocked to discover that the world was actually run by inter-dimensional shape-shifting lizard people from a rip in the space-time continuum. Icke's findings had been rejected by old-fashioned conventional academics, but when he'd shown pictures of world leaders with slightly enlarged pupils, Blandon had seen all the proof he needed.

But could David Icke have killed Professor Companion? Maybe he'd discovered the professor was a shape-shifting lizard too.

No, it didn't make sense. His shape-shifting lizard guts would have been visible in his open stomach.

'I don't think it could be,' said Blandon. 'We're at a dead end.'

Blandon collapsed to the floor and held his head in his hands. Blood from his wound gushed down into his eyes.

As soon as the police puzzleology department worked out the clue was an anagram, Fascist would find him. And then he'd have more than a severe head wound to worry about.

Florence fixed her prematurely wise eyes at the sculpture and sifted through her keen brain for clues.

Michelangelo.

*Michelangelo.*

**Michelangelo.**

Michelangelo.

She'd heard someone else say the name recently, but who? Of course.

She'd overheard Inspector Fascist saying it.

'I've just remembered something,' cried Florence. 'Something Fascist told his puzzleology department on the phone. He said that while you were unconscious in the hospital, you'd been chanting the names "Leonardo, Michelangelo and

Donatello" over and over again.'

Blandon leapt to his feet.

Florence was right.

The words 'Leonardo, Michelangelo and Donatello' were in the back of his big mind. Was this what he'd been talking about with Professor Companion?

Leonardo.

Michelangelo.

Donatello.

*What was the link?*

A vision of stone faces gazing out across a narrow courtyard from neat alcoves flitted into Blandon's mind.

'The courtyard of the Uffizi Gallery!' shouted Blandon. 'There are statues of Leonardo, Michelangelo and Donatello there. That must be the place your father was really sending us.'

Blandon wiped the blood out of his eyes and started to run.


## Chapter 14

The assassin jumped off her BMW motorbike and thundered over to the courtyard. It was time to embrace the glory of the night.

*The night she had prepared for.*

She had been lost for so long.

*In the middle of the journey of life I found myself within a dark woods where the straight way was lost,* she thought, intelligently quoting Dante to herself.

She had spent so long in hell, so long climbing the mountain of purgatory and now it was time to ascend to the celestial spheres of heaven.

Soon her task would be over. And her transformation from shade to saint would be complete.

She'd spent so long frozen in the lake of ignorance.

Burning in the fires of incomprehension.

Trapped in the overturned vehicle of untruth with no mobile signal and an agonizing back injury.

Then one day, while she was glancing at an Internet message board, she came across the Pathfinder.

Finally, she had stumbled on the truth.

She'd begged the Pathfinder to let her join the organization.

*He'd refused.*

But she gave up her job, her house, her hair, everything.

She even bought a cool motorcycle.

*That's how serious she was.*

The organization had accepted her.

The Pathfinder had told her the truth about every unexplained event in history:

The rise of the Illuminati.

The secret bloodline of Christ.

The assassination of JFK.

The popularity of Coldplay.

It all became clear. When the Pathfinder revealed his plans for this great night, she accepted without question.

*This was her gift.*

*This was her inferno.*

## Chapter 15

Dr Allan Allard from the Florence University puzzleology department waited in the museum courtyard. He had gentle brown eyes, an aggressive moustache and a beard that radiated intelligence. He was wearing Harris Tweed, a black turtleneck sweater, khaki trousers and Somerset loafers. But it's not really worth remembering any of that stuff because he's going to die in a few seconds.

He'd been waiting over an hour for Robert Blandon and still there was no sign of him. Professor Companion had told him to come here and guide Blandon to safety if he was brutally murdered.

*I'll guide Blandon to you with some cryptic clues,* he'd said. *There's bound to be time to write them if I've been brutally murdered.*

Could it be possible that the great Blandon had failed to solve the clues?

'Dammit, I'm mad,' muttered Dr Allan Allard to himself. He was the head of the faculty's palindromes department and everything he ever said was the same backwards as forwards.

He looked down at the floor. Someone had dumped a cigar there, even though the bin was only a few feet away.

'Cigar? Toss it in a can. It is so tragic,' he muttered to himself.

Something moved in the distance.

'Was it a car or a cat I saw?' he asked himself.

It was neither. Someone was walking towards him.

*At last.* Blandon had followed the trail and it was time to take him to safety.

He seemed to have had an image change, though. Dr Allan

Allard was used to seeing Blandon wearing tweed jackets and turtleneck sweaters, just like any other puzzleologist. But today he seemed to be wearing a body-hugging leather biker suit.

But no. This wasn't Blandon at all. It was a woman.

'Madam?' asked Allard.

Instead of replying, the woman reached into her pocket and pulled out a handgun.

Dr Allan Allard didn't run. He knew his time had come.

He simply looked his assassin in the eye and said, 'Draw, o coward!'

## Chapter 16

The world-famous Uffizi Gallery was first opened to the public in 1765. You can visit from 8:15 to 18:50 Tuesday to Sunday. Tickets cost €9.50, including a discount voucher for the local Hard Rock Café. It's worth getting there early on weekends and during the summer holidays to avoid queues. A rooftop café serving light snacks and coffee offers fantastic views across the city.

Blandon turned into the narrow courtyard and looked up at the statues lining the façade. As well as Leonardo, Michelangelo and Donatello, there were other great Florentines such as Machiavelli, Galileo, da Vinci, Boccaccio and Dante Alighieri.

Blandon's clever eyes stopped on this last statue.

Dante Alighieri. Author of The Divine Comedy.

Something was forcing its way into his injured brain.

Of course!

He'd been reading the first part of that epic poem last

night, while he was waiting for Professor Companion.

*Inferno.*

He'd bought it at the airport bookshop.

He'd been browsing the puzzleology section when a couple of overexcited fans had spotted him and demanded that he sign their copies of *Wordsearches and the Knights Templar*. He'd scribbled his best wishes and sneaked out of the shop before more eager fans could snoop at him. On his way out, he'd grabbed a copy of *The Divine Comedy*.

But where was the book now?

'Look over there,' urged Florence.

She pointed to someone lying on the ground at the far end of the courtyard.

'That must be the person my dad sent to help us,' said Florence. 'I expect they're having a quick nap while they wait for us.'

Blandon was about to run over to the body when he saw another figure walking towards him.

With a gun.

A 9mm Glock 17 Gen 4.

'What the hell?' asked Blandon.

'Run!' shouted Florence.


**Chapter 17**


Bang.

## Chapter 18

The assassin fired her gun over and over again.

*Damn.*

*Missed.*

Soon she was out of bullets and Blandon and his companion were gone.

She'd managed to miss them both at close range.

It didn't matter.

Let the fool live for now.

She had things to get on with.

*And by 'things' she meant murders.*

The assassin stalked back to Dr Allard's body and flipped it over. Using her strong arms, she grabbed his head and twisted it all the way round.

Crack!

Now he would look the wrong way for eternity. A fitting punishment for someone who'd tried to peer into the secrets of the organization.

The assassin was about to walk away when something occurred to her.

She had an idea about how to keep the police off her scent for even longer.

She dipped her finger into Dr Allan Allard's bullet wound, pulled it out and began to write.

## Chapter 19

Inspector Fascist darted towards the Uffizi courtyard. His angry heart was pumping angry blood in his chest and his breath was angry and short, but he didn't care. He was about to close in on the famous Robert Blandon.

He had been heading back to the station when Giuseppe from the police puzzleology department had radioed him.

'I've had a breakthrough on "Mega hell icon",' he had said. 'I don't think it's about a big hell painting at all. I think it's an anagram.'

'Slow down, egghead,' Fascist had barked. 'I'm out in the field chasing a killer and all you can do is fill my head with jargon.'

'Sorry,' said Giuseppe. 'It's the name for when you rearrange the letters of a word or phrase to make a new one.'

'And that's what we pay you for, is it?' he had snorted. 'Rearranging letters?'

'Sorry,' said Giuseppe. 'But I really think I'm on to something. You can arrange the letters "Mega hell icon" into "Michelangelo". That's where I think Blandon's gone. To somewhere associated with Michelangelo.'

Fascist had slammed his radio down in disgust.

These college boys were all the same. Sitting behind their desks using fancy words like 'anagram' and leaving him to chase dangerous killers like Blandon.

Since his precious little puzzleologist had had his brainwave, he'd been on a wild goose chase that had taken in the replica of David outside the Palazza Vecchio, the Piazzale Michelangelo in the Oltrano district, and the Michelangelo hotel on Viale Fratelli Rosselli.

But this time he was sure he'd come to the right place.

He turned the corner into the narrow courtyard.

Someone was lying on the floor in the far corner.

It was a body.

*A dead body*.

But Blandon was nowhere to be seen.

A wave of sickness crashed onto the rocks of Fascist's mind as he approached the body. It had been twisted, mutilated.

*And there was a message on the floor next to it.*


## Chapter 20

Blandon looked over his shoulder. There was no one on the street.

'I think we've outpaced them,' said Florence. 'But where should we go now?'

'I don't know,' said Blandon. 'I need some time to think.'

He felt the wound on the back of his head. The blood was still pouring out thick and fast.

'Well, get on with it,' said Florence. 'I reckon that person my father sent to help us wasn't sleeping at all. I think they were dead.'

Dead?

Blandon thought about it.

The man had been lying down.

He'd seen someone with a gun.

It made a lot of sense.

Someone *or something* had killed him.

Probably someone rather than something, actually.

But who?

Fascist?

A killer working for a mysterious organization?

'Think about the words you were chanting,' said Florence. 'Could they have been pointing us somewhere else?'

Something in the back of Blandon's mind was trying to help him. *But what?*

A memory forced its way into the front of Blandon's brain.

He'd gone out for a drink with his students to celebrate their graduation last year. They'd ended up in a hip hop bar, where local disadvantaged youngsters were taking part in rap battles.

Blandon had been fascinated by the symbology of the place. He wondered if the boisterous young men in the crowded bar knew that the gesture of miming a sideways gun with your fingers was originally used by the Knights Templar. Or that the practice of wearing your jeans lower than your underpants had its roots in Freemasonry.

He was so caught up in clever thought he hardly noticed when a young man in a hooded sweater grabbed him and pulled him up on stage to battle the reigning champion.

As the dope beat kicked in behind him, Blandon had tried to explain that he was merely an observer. The audience turned to him as one and held their hands around their necks in a 'choking' mime.

Blandon tried to explain that this gesture had its origins in the Priory of Sion, when he found that the words coming out of his mouth were fitting the beat perfectly. And they were rhyming too.

He was rapping.

No, he wasn't just rapping. He was spitting out rhymes with tight flow.

*He was a natural.*

The crowd went wild, trippin' with fever for the Blandon flava.

Soon all the other sucker MCs were defeated and Blandon was crowned champion.

*But why was he remembering this now?*

What did it have to do with his current situation?

Leonardo.

Michelangelo.

Donatello.

The words came back into Blandon's mind.

But this time he wasn't just listing them. He was rapping them.

*Leonardo*

*Michelangelo*

*And Donatello*

*Make up the team with one other fella*

*Raphael.*

He hadn't been chanting in his sleep last night. *He'd been rapping.*

Blandon stopped in his tracks as it came back to him:

'T-U-R-T-L-E Power!'

It hadn't been Renaissance artists he'd been thinking about. He'd been remembering the words to the 1991 hit 'Turtle Power' by Partners in Kryme. He'd been thinking about the *Teenage Mutant Ninja Turtles.*

He hadn't been telling himself to go to the Uffizi courtyard. He'd been telling himself to go down into the sewers. That's where Professor Companion had sent someone to help them.

## Chapter 21

Fascist yanked his phone out of his pocket and punched a number into it.

He waited for that idiot Giuseppe to pick up.

'Did you find Blandon at the square?' asked Giuseppe.

'No,' woofed Fascist. 'But he's been here all right. We

found another body on the scene. That means we're looking at a double murder now.'

Giuseppe gasped.

*Double murder was the worst crime this side of triple murder.*

'How did he kill this one?' asked Giuseppe.

'Looks like he shot him and twisted his head round,' said Fascist.

Fascist heard a soft sob from the other end of the line.

He snorted in reply. If this jumped-up little bookworm didn't have the stomach for police work, he should never have got into it.

'One more thing,' said Fascist. 'The dead guy wrote a message in blood just before he died. I need you to tell me what it means, and this time I want results fast. Do you have a pen?'

'Yes, sir,' said Giuseppe.

'Okay,' said Fascist. 'Here's the message. "Robert Blandon killed me. He's the one that did it. Just to make myself absolutely clear, I was murdered by Robert Blandon, that American guy with the mullet who runs around between touristy locations with attractive female companions."'


## Chapter 22

Fascist fished his phone out of his pocket. It was that idiot Giuseppe. This time he'd better have some results.

'What have you got on the message?' growled Fascist.

'We're still working on that,' said Giuseppe. 'But we've found a link between the two murders. Both Professor Companion and Dr Allan Allard were arranged on the floor to reflect the shades in Dante's *Inferno*.'

'What?' yapped Fascist. 'I don't have time to listen to this mumbo jumbo.'

'*Inferno*,' simpered Giuseppe apologetically. 'It's part of an epic poem called *The Divine Comedy*. It's one of the books we keep here in the department.'

Fascist rolled his eyes and mouth.

*A book.* He'd tried reading one of those on holiday once. *Total waste of time.*

It was just a list of things that happened and stuff people said. Like a film or TV show you had to imagine for yourself.

He was so incensed he'd taken his handgun out of his swimming trunks and unloaded it into the ridiculous object.

If these filmmakers were too lazy to record things, he was damned if he was going to waste his holiday imagining stuff for them.

'And there's one more thing,' attempted Giuseppe. 'One of your men found a book in the pocket of Blandon's tweed jacket when he was admitted to the hospital last night. It turns out it was *Inferno*. Dante's *Inferno*.'

'Blandon!' shouted Fascist at the top of his voice.

He threw his phone to the ground, stamped on it, shouted 'Blandon' again, then bent down, picked his phone up and wiped the dirt off.

This had gone too far.

When he finally caught up with that tweedy douchebag, he'd shoot first and ask questions later.

In fact, he probably wouldn't bother with the questions at all.

## Chapter 23

Blandon waded through the thick brown liquid of the ancient sewer. The smell of decay, death and human waste fondled his eyes and nostrils.

*The smell from his dream.*

'Are you sure this is the place you were telling yourself to go?' asked Florence. 'I bought these loafers just last week and they're pretty much ruined now.'

'I'm sure,' asserted Blandon, forcing himself on through the dark, narrow tunnel.

Dark.

Narrow.

*Narrow.*

'It's fine,' barked Blandon.

He was in fact blustering to cover an acute sense of claustrophobia rooted in childhood.

*He was seven years old.*

*It had been a bright sunny day.*

*He'd been playing in the fields with his friends. He'd spent the last three hours telling them all about the hidden Masonic symbolism in Washington DC. He'd told them about every single one of the shapes you could trace over the street maps, and the secret messages they revealed. It had been a great day. But suddenly, they'd all accidentally pushed him down a well.*

*He was falling.*

*Falling.*

*Plunging into an icy blackness.*

*Cold.*

*He cried out for help, but his friends had all accidentally walked away.*

*Cold.*

*Alone.*

*He was trapped in the freezing darkness for twenty-four hours, gazing up at the circle of light above his head.*

*At one point the moon passed into the dead centre. Blandon chuckled to himself as he thought about how few people would know this resembled the circumpunct, a symbol with important meaning for ancient Egyptian religion, Eastern philosophy and the Kabbalah. He couldn't wait to get out and tell his friends about it.*

*Eventually, a rescue team arrived and pulled him up to safety. They were shocked by his stamina and strength of mind. And they were fascinated to hear about the symbology of the circumpunct.*

*His friends accidentally forgot to apologize when he saw them, but Blandon could tell they were overjoyed.*

*The* Boston Globe *had run a front-page story headlined 'Young Symbology Genius Survives Night Trapped in Well'.*

*Blandon had been hailed as a hero.*

*But he suffered chronic claustrophobia to this day, which made him dread the inevitable underground passageway sequences in his adventures.*

Blandon snapped out of the flashback and the font switched out of italics.

He told himself to relax.

To keep it together.

The last thing he needed was a panic attack on top of the chronic blood loss.

He had to trudge on, even as the copper smell of the blood flowing from his head mixed with the sharp diarrhoea tang of the liquid at his feet.

Words floated through his smart head:

*I saw people smothered in a filth that out of human privies seemed to flow.*

Where were they from?
Had he used them in his rap battle?
No, he'd read them yesterday.
They were from *Inferno*.
*Dante's* Inferno.
Blandon's foot stomped on something hard.
A rat?
If so, it was a six-foot-long rat wearing a tweed jacket.
Blandon reached down into the sewage and flipped the object over. It was a body.
A *dead* body.
Florence screamed.

## Chapter 24

Fascist trudged through the narrow tunnel. The sewage was seeping into his shoes. If this was Giuseppe's idea of a joke, he wouldn't think twice about pinning both the murders on him and looking the other way while angry members of the public tore him to pieces.

Giuseppe had called him while he was on the way back to the station.

'I've got something,' he said. 'There's a bit in this book where the bodies of sinners are floating in a pit of shit. I think this means Blandon will strike in the sewers next.'

Fascist had listened out for the sound of giggling on the other end of the line, but there was nothing. The little twerp was serious.

Well, where was the tweed-clad killer?

Fascist had been down here for ten minutes and he hadn't seen him yet.

It sickened him to think of those pampered little fools in his puzzleology department reading books with their feet up while he waded through all this filth. Just because they could do hard puzzles and he couldn't.

What was the big deal about puzzles anyway?

When he'd been a boy, he'd been taught that bravery, strength and honour were the most important things in the world. But these things meant nothing to the youth of today. They just wanted to waste their time listening to idiots like Blandon drone on about crosswords, Boggle and Madlibs.

It made him sick.

A scream echoed down the smelly corridor.

*A woman.*

Blandon was on the attack again.

He drew his pistol out of his pocket and fired it down the tunnel.

## Chapter 25

The body had a gentle mouth, a keen nose and blue eyes that radiated intelligence and deadness. He was wearing a Harris Tweed jacket, a black turtleneck, khaki trousers and loafers.

*He's one of us*, thought Blandon. *A puzzleologist.*

'I recognize him,' sobbed Florence. 'That's Mr TV Quiz Jock Bags Few Lynx PhD. He ran the pangram department at my father's faculty.'

'Looks like they got to him before us,' said Blandon.

*I saw people smothered in a filth that out of human privies seemed to flow.*

It was like something out of Dante's *Inferno*.

Gunshots echoed in the narrow tunnel behind them.

'What the hell?' blurted Blandon.

'Quick!' shouted Florence. 'Run!'

## Chapter 26

Fascist kicked over the body that was bobbing about in the sewage. It was another of those puzzleology types. This was Blandon's work all right.

He didn't have a problem with these puzzleologists killing each other. The sooner the world was rid of them, the better. But why did they have to do it on his patch?

He'd happily let these fools kill each other, rip their guts out and arrange them into clues resembling ancient symbols all day long if it weren't for the paperwork.

The paperwork for any enigmatic symbology-themed murders was a bitch.

He was going to put a stop to all this nonsense.

And he was going to do it now.

He drew his pistol out of his pocket again and fired it down the tunnel in case Blandon was still there.

## Chapter 27

Blandon slumped down in the darkness of the doorway. They'd emerged from the sewers on the Via dei Benci and cowered in the darkness, fearing police patrols.

'We've followed all the clues,' said Blandon. 'Everyone your father sent to help us has been killed. We might as well turn ourselves in.'

'There must be other clues,' said Florence. 'My father always left clues.'

She remembered her fifteenth birthday, when her father had set up an elaborate series of puzzles leading to her present. She'd solved riddles, unravelled anagrams and decoded secret messages in famous works of art before finding her present.

Even now she could remember tearing back the wrapping paper to reveal the black and white photograph of a man who looked like either Harrison Ford or Tom Hanks.

It was Robert Blandon's first book, *Holy See of Tranquillity*, which used trigonomic evidence to prove the Catholic Church had faked the moon landings.

Florence spent the rest of the day devouring the book. By the time she'd finished, she knew she wanted to be a puzzleologist.

This wasn't the boring history she'd been taught in school, where you had to compare sources and weigh up evidence. This was a different kind of history. One where you drew far-fetched connections between unrelated events in books that were sold in the same shops as scented candles and crystal healing packs.

Blandon had been the man who'd inspired her to get involved in this worthwhile field of study. And now it was up to her to protect him.

She wracked her brain, which was almost as clever as Blandon's.

She had spotted something else on the picture of her dead dad.

Something that might have been a clue.

She took the picture out of her pocket.

Just below his neck and above the large cut in his torso, her father had traced a tiny squiggle of blood.

Florence thrust the photo towards Blandon.

'What do you make of this?' she asked. 'Do you think it's a symbol?'

Blandon snatched the photo and peered at it. An icy chill swept through his blood.

It was a symbol all right.

It was one of the most famous symbols of all.

*The rose.*

And he'd painted it in blood in the middle of his outstretched arms, turning his entire body into a cross with a rose in the centre.

The symbol of the world's deadliest secret society.

*The Rosicrucians.*

The Knights of the Rose Cross.


## Chapter 28

'So what do you have to say for yourself?' barked the authoritative man. He had spiteful eyes, a mean nose, selfish cheeks, malicious eyebrows and a vindictive chin.

'I'm sorry,' said Fascist. 'We're doing the best we can.'

He was standing in the office of his boss, Lieutenant Despot. Police awards stared intimidatingly down from the shelves.

'The best you can?' thundered Despot. 'Three puzzle-ologists have died tonight. Is that the best you can do?'

Fascist looked down at his feet. His blood was boiling.

What was he supposed to do? Blandon could solve any riddle in half the time it took his pea-brained puzzleology department. How was he supposed to compete against him with those fools on his team?

Fascist said nothing.

Giuseppe from the puzzleology department was Lieutenant Despot's nephew. That's why he got to relax in his precious office all day long while Fascist had to get his hands dirty catching murderers.

'This Blandon is making a mockery of us,' said Despot. 'As soon as he touches down in Italy, he thinks he can start murdering whoever he pleases, just because he's rich and famous. Well, we need to show him that we won't stand for it.'

'Yes, sir,' said Fascist.

'Now get out of this building and don't return until you're carrying Blandon's corpse,' said Despot. 'Any more mistakes and you can forget about promotion.'

## Chapter 29

'Who are the Rosicrucians?' asked Florence.

Blandon took a deep breath.

'They're a society formed by a German monk called Christian Rosenkreuz in the fifteenth century. He collected occult wisdom that had been guarded throughout the ages and shared it with followers, giving them secret insight into the spiritual realm.'

'I think I've heard of them,' said Florence. 'Wasn't the whole thing revealed to be a massive hoax?'

'Yes,' said Blandon. 'But in a way that just reveals how true it all was.'

Florence nodded. It made a lot of sense.

'So why did my dad want to remind us of the Rosicrucians?' asked Florence.

Blandon's blood ran cold, then boiled, then ran cold again. This was the bit he'd been dreading.

'I think they killed your father,' he sighed. 'I think he was getting too close to the truth about them and they decided to take him out of the picture. I once used the Fibonacci Sequence to prove they'd been responsible for the fluoridation of the water supply. Maybe your dad was about to go public with something big like that.'

Florence nodded. Blandon noticed her eyes were moist with frightened tears.

'Maybe we should go to the police,' she cooed. 'They're bound to understand if we explain it to them.'

'No,' said Blandon. It was too late for that now.

*Far too late.*

By running from the police, they'd crossed a line.

*At the speed of light.*

Plus, he was sure there was something more to the professor's message.

Something he was missing.

Rose.

Cross.

There were no Rosicrucian headquarters in Florence.

At least, *none that he knew of.*

*Rose.*

*Cross.*

'Of course!' shouted Blandon, leaping to his feet. 'Why didn't I think of it? There's a very famous rose cross just a couple of streets away from us.'

Florence stared at him, her eyes still stinging with hurtful memories.

'The *rose* window of the Basilica of the Holy *Cross*,' asserted Blandon.

'Of course,' agreed Florence.

She leapt to her feet and they raced away.

## Chapter 30

*Dying. I'm dying.*

Renowned puzzleologist Dr Kakuro staggered across Piazza Sante Croce. His thick black hair and small, clever eyes shook back and forth as he zigzagged across the picturesque square. He stumbled forward, wrestling the searing pain in his heart.

*Dying.*

*Soon I'll be dead.*

He looked up at the renowned neogothic façade of the Basilica of the Holy Cross, the largest Franciscan church in the world. He thought about the sixteen chapels inside, some of which were decorated with frescos by Giotto, and his pupil Taddeo Gaddi. He thought about how the church had got its name from the splinter of holy cross that was donated to the Franciscans by King Louis of France in 1258.

*Dying.*

*My life is ending.*

He thought about all the famous Florentines buried inside. Michelangelo, Machiavelli, Galileo. He thought about the large, empty sarcophagus awaiting the body of Dante Alighieri.

*Dying.*

*My life is draining away.*

Dante was buried in Ravenna, where he died in 1321.

Florence had made many requests for his remains, but they'd all been refused. In 1829, they'd even built the elaborate tomb inside the Basilica of Santa Croce, but it remained empty to this day.

*Dying.*

*These are my final moments.*

The beauty of the Basilica of the Holy Cross so overwhelmed the French writer Stendhal (the pen name of Marie-Henri Beyle) that he suffered from fierce heart palpitations. He gave his name to Stendhal Syndrome, a psychosomatic disorder causing faintness and dizziness when an individual is exposed to beautiful works of art.

But Dr Kakuro wasn't suffering from Stendhal Syndrome now.

He was dying.

*Dying.*

*This is almost it now.*

## Chapter 31

The assassin watched the tweed-jacketed man stagger back and forth across the piazza. Another enemy of the organization was dead.

*And she had something special lined up for him.*

She dashed back to her motorbike and opened the storage compartment. She took out a trowel, a bottle of lighter fluid and some matches.

As she strode aggressively back to the piazza, she thought back to her early days in the organization.

*I found myself within a dark woods where the straight way was lost.*

She'd had so much to learn.

One day the Pathfinder had produced an American dollar bill.

'What can you tell me about this?' he'd asked.

'It's the one-dollar bill,' she'd said. 'It shows George Washington on one side and the Great Seal of the United States on the other side.'

'Good,' he said. 'But what if I told you it was covered in secret symbology?'

She'd narrowed her eyes at him. She was hoping this would make her look suspicious, but it actually just made her look tired, so she opened them fully again.

The Pathfinder had pointed to the pyramid on the Great Seal. 'A blazing eye on the top of a large stone structure. Where have you seen that before?'

'*Lord of the Rings*?' she'd attempted.

The Pathfinder had smiled and shook his head. 'It's the all-seeing eye, the symbol that proves the deadliest secret society of all, the Illuminati, are watching over us.'

Next, he pointed to the Latin phrase 'Novos Ordo Seculorum' and asked 'What do you think this means?'

'Novos... Ordos... Seculorum,' she'd muttered. 'My Latin is a little rusty. Does it mean "a new order for the ages"? A reference to the fourth Eclogue of Virgil?'

'Close,' the master had said. 'It actually means "new world order". It's a threat from the tiny handful of people who really run the world. They want to form a world government and enslave everyone.'

She'd gasped when she'd heard this.

Shock had been her reaction then.

*Anger was her reaction now.*

'You're telling me all this is on the one-dollar bill?' she'd panted.

'The truth is hidden in plain sight,' the Pathfinder had said. 'Like it always is.'

Then he said to her, 'Now count the number of steps on the unfinished pyramid, the number of stars on the eagle's head, the number of stripes on its shield and the number of letters in the phrase "Annuit Coeptus".'

She'd counted them again and again.

*Was she going crazy?*

They all had exactly the same number.

*The number thirteen.*

'That refers to Friday 13 October 1307, the day King Philip IV of France ordered the arrest of the Knight's Templar,' said the Pathfinder.

'The Knight's Templar?' she'd protested. 'Another secret society hidden on the dollar bill?'

'That's not all,' he said. 'The deadliest secret society of all is also mentioned.'

He grabbed a pen and traced a Star of David over the seal's pyramid. It highlighted the letters 'a', 's', 'n', 'o' and 'm' from the surrounding motto.

Asnom.

*An anagram of Mason.*

He turned the bill around and pointed to the man on the front. 'And on the front you'll find one of the most famous masons of all, George Washington.'

It was all becoming clear to her now. The Illuminati, Masons and Knights Templar were revealing their agenda of world domination on the most famous banknote on earth, knowing that only really clever people would pick up on it, while the ordinary sheeple went about their everyday lives, oblivious to the unseen powers controlling them.

Then the Pathfinder explained it all to her.

He told her what was really going on.

That's when she decided to dedicate her life to the cause.

Even if it meant dying for it.

## Chapter 32

*Dying. I'm dying.*

Renowned nearly-dead puzzleologist Dr Kakuro collapsed onto the ground in the Piazza Santa Croce. He was in charge of the number puzzle department at the faculty, and had been working on a really hard Su Doku when Professor Companion had called.

'I need you to wait outside the Basilica of the Holy Cross tonight,' he had said.

'Can't it wait?' Kakuro had asked. 'I'm just about to finish a really difficult Su Doku.'

'I wish it could,' said Professor Companion. 'But I need you to help protect the greatest puzzleologist in the world. Robert Blandon.'

Kakuro had dropped his Su Doku book, pencil and jaw.

'Robert Blandon?' he'd spluttered. 'Blandon might be in danger?'

Kakuro would have done anything in the world to help Blandon. If it weren't for Blandon, he'd never have become a puzzleologist.

*It was as simple as that.*

He'd been an eight-year-old child living in Tokyo when his father had returned home with the Japanese translation of Blandon's *Protractor of the Gods*.

In it, Blandon used the Pythagorean Theorem to prove that all the ancient civilizations of earth had been established by aliens.

When Kakuro had finished the convincing, respected academic book, he'd gazed at the author photo on the inside jacket. There was Robert Blandon, with his Harris Tweed, his black turtleneck, his gently probing eyes, his sternly intelligent lips, his deeply authoritative voice, his carefree athletic smile and his thick brown mullet, flecked with grey hairs that sang of wisdom and renownedness.

The next day, when he came down to dinner, he'd grown a mullet of his own, and he was wearing a child's-size tweed jacket, a black turtleneck and a child's pair of loafers.

That's how much he'd wanted to become Blandon.

His father spat sushi angrily onto the table and his mother had cried in anguish.

'You have brought shame on us,' they cried.

But Kakuro didn't care.

He just wanted to devote his life to puzzleology. To the study of secret, mystical knowledge and alternate history that were hidden away from all those who refused to see, and those who had even the slightest idea what they were on about.

Now he was dying.

*Dying.*

*Almost dead.*

A bullet had come out of the dark shadows and embedded itself in his heart, with searing, icy heat.

*He was dying.*

But at least he'd died trying to protect Robert Blandon.

His idol.

*But I am not dead yet*, he thought.

Dipping his finger into his barely pumping heart, he began to write on the cold stones of the piazza.

*I am not dead yet.*

He would save Blandon with another puzzle, a final puzzle that would stand as his final work, his greatest work.

*I am not dead yet.*

He traced out the letters on the ground one by one, safe in the knowledge that his short life would not have been in vain if he could save the great Robert Blandon.

*I am not dead yet.*

Dipping his finger deep into his heart, he finished the puzzle, his final masterpiece.

*I am not dead yet.*

*Oh, actually I am now.*

Dr Kakuro's body fell still as the assassin paced towards it.


## Chapter 33

'What the hell?' shouted Blandon.

He saw a flickering light in the middle of the Piazza Santa Croce.

Underneath it was a body.

Or more accurately, *part of a body*.

One of the paving stones had been wrenched up and a deep vertical pit had been hollowed.

The body was inside the pit, with just its feet and calves sticking out.

Blandon could see from the khaki trousers and loafers that it was another puzzleologist.

Flames were rising up from the soles of the loafers. Someone had set them on fire.

'Is he dead?' sobbed Florence.

Blandon prodded the leg. There was no response. He nodded at the weeping female puzzleology grad.

'I think that's Dr Kakuro from my father's faculty,' said Florence. 'They must have been onto something big to make the Rosicrucians kill them all.'

*No kidding,* thought Blandon. *But what?*

He stared at the body.

Words floated through his renowned mind.

*Out of the mouth of each one there protruded the feet of a transgressor, and the legs up to the calf.*

He'd been reading these words recently. But where?

*The rest within remained. In all of them the soles were both on fire.*

They were from Dante's *Inferno*. In the eighth circle of hell, those guilty of simony were buried headfirst in pits, with eternal flames lapping their feet.

Whoever was killing the puzzleologists must also have been a Dante fan. But why had they chosen to murder one of them so close to the intended resting place of the poet?

Blandon stared up at the façade of the Basilica of the Holy Cross. He'd often chuckle to himself when he saw American tourists taking pictures of Dante's tomb.

*That's not where his body is,* his superior brain would think.

But now there was a body. The body of an innocent puzzleology professor. And his corpse referenced Dante's *Inferno*.

*What did it all mean?*

'What does it all mean?' asked Blandon.

'I think this might be a clue,' said Florence.

*She thought it might be a clue.*

Florence pointed to the floor with an unsteady finger. 'What the hell?' asked Blandon.

## Chapter 34

A few metres away from the pit where he was buried, Dr Kakuro had scrawled some numbers in his own blood:

| 37 | 78 | 29 | 70 | 21 | 62 | 13 | 54 | 5 |
|----|----|----|----|----|----|----|----|----|
| 6 | 38 | 79 | 30 | 71 | 22 | 63 | 14 | 46 |
| 47 | 7 | 39 | 80 | 31 | 72 | 23 | 55 | 15 |
| 16 | 48 | 8 | 40 | 81 | 32 | 64 | 24 | 56 |
| 57 | 17 | 49 | 9 | 41 | 73 | 33 | 65 | 25 |
| 26 | 58 | 18 | 50 | 1 | 42 | 74 | 34 | 66 |
| 67 | 27 | 59 | 10 | 51 | 2 | 43 | 75 | 35 |
| 36 | 68 | 19 | 60 | 11 | 52 | 3 | 44 | 76 |
| 77 | 28 | 69 | 20 | 61 | 12 | 53 | 4 | 45 |

'The poor man,' said Florence. 'He must have got bored waiting to die and decided to play Su Doku. It makes sense. I know how much he used to love it.'

'I guess you're right,' said Blandon. He turned to walk away from the numbers, but a thought popped into his Harvard brain that made his blood run cold as it trickled out of his head wound.

'Wait a minute!' he shouted. 'Su Doku squares feature only the numbers one through nine. This features the numbers one through eighty-one.'

Florence gasped.

'Maybe it's a message,' she cried. 'He could be telling us where to go next!'

Blandon stared at the scrawl.

Was it a cypher, with each number standing for a letter of the alphabet?

No. There were only twenty-six letters in the alphabet.

*Unless Kakuro had been using extra secret letters the government had been hiding from us.*

He wasn't sure what the point of those would be, though.

It was something to do with the way the numbers were arranged.

Blandon concentrated on the numbers, ignoring the searing pain from his gushing wound.

He added up all the numbers on the top row. He didn't even need to grab a piece of paper and jot the numbers down. He just did it in his head. That's how clever his Ivy League brain was.

$$37 + 78 + 29 + 70 + 21 + 62 + 13 + 54 + 5 = 369$$

Next, he added up the numbers down the first column. He didn't even have to say the numbers out loud as he did it.

$$37 + 6 + 47 + 16 + 57 + 26 + 67 + 36 + 77 = 369$$

Next, he tried the numbers running diagonally in both directions. They came to the same number.

'That isn't a Su Doku grid at all,' gasped Blandon. 'It's a magic square.'

Florence shot Blandon a glance of suspicion.

*Had the great puzzleologist lost his mind?*

Blandon chuckled.

'I don't mean it's a square with magical powers,' he reassured. 'A "magic square" is a mathematical term for a grid of consecutive numbers where all the rows, columns and diagonals add up to the same sum.'

Florence peered down at the square and added up the numbers. She couldn't do it as quickly as Blandon, but she could still do it without a calculator, which was very smart.

'That's amazing,' said Florence. At school she'd found maths boring, but it had really come to life for her now it was part of this deadly treasure hunt. Maybe she'd get her old times tables out when this whole nightmare was over.

*If it was over*, she thought glumly.

*What had Dr Kakuro meant?* wondered Blandon, who was also thinking.

Magic squares.

*Of course*, thought Blandon. *Paolo dell'Abbaco.* He was a fourteenth-century mathematician who'd written about magic squares in his book *Tratto d'Abbaco.*

He'd also been the tutor of Dante's son Jacopo.

*Dante Alighieri.*

*Inferno.*

*There it was again.*

He was buried at the Santa Trinita church, just a few streets away.

'We need to get to the Santa Trinita,' shouted Blandon. 'Fast.'

## Chapter 35

Fascist ran into the Piazza Santa Croce and saw the burning legs sticking out of the hole. He tried to kick them in frustration, but only ended up setting his own trousers on fire.

Blandon had made a fool of him again. His own useless puzzleology department had sent him to the banks of the Arno River. Apparently one of the scenes in that stupid book had been set on a riverbank.

It turned out to be another wild goose chase.

Fascist had heard a gunshot from the direction of the Santa Croce church, but by the time he'd got there, the murderous American puzzleologist had fled again.

He yanked his phone angrily from his pocket.

'Hi, Inspector Fascist,' said Giuseppe lazily.

'Turns out your river idea was a crock of shit,' roared Fascist. 'While I was wasting my time down there, Blandon was busy murdering in the Piazza Santa Croce. He even had the time to bury his victim in the ground with just his legs sticking out and then to set fire to his feet.'

'Oh yeah,' squeaked Giuseppe. 'That happens in the book as well, come to think of it.'

Fascist couldn't believe his ears. All this pampered idiot had to do was read a book and he couldn't even do that properly. He opened his mouth to scream his head off but it fell limp as he spotted something.

Fascist's eyes bulged out of their sockets.

A grid of numbers had been scrawled on the pavement beneath him.

It was a puzzle.

'I've got something for you,' said Fascist. 'And this time you'd better come through.'

## Chapter 36

Florence grabbed Blandon and shoved him into a dark doorway, pressing herself against his buff lecturer's body.

'Isn't it a little early for this?' he protested. 'I haven't even defeated the baddies yet.'

'Quiet,' she hissed, and pointed across the street, where Fascist was stomping like an antagonized muskrat. 'Keep still.'

Blandon watched Fascist charge off down the street.

Florence took the Polaroid of her dead father out of her pocket and stared at it again. There was something still bothering her about it. Something she couldn't quite place.

*There it was.*

In the top right-hand corner of the picture she could see her father's left eye enclosed in a triangle of blood. After he'd ripped his body open, scrawled the riddle, done the Michelangelo anagram and drawn the rose on his chest, he must have daubed a triangle of blood on the floor, plucked his eye out and placed it inside.

*But why?*

What was he trying to tell them?

'What do you make of this?' she asked Blandon, pointing to the eye and triangle on the Polaroid. 'Do you think my father's eye fell out as he was dying?'

Blandon's heart raced, speeding the flow of blood from his head wound.

'I think he put it there on purpose,' gasped Blandon. 'And I think he was trying to tell us something.'

'Something about what happened to him,' said Blandon, who was still speaking.

'That's the all-seeing eye,' spluttered Blandon, still the person talking.

'It's the symbol of the Illuminati,' said Blandon, who hadn't shut up yet.

'The Illuminati?' asked Florence.

'The deadliest secret society in the world,' said Blandon. 'Ever heard of a man called Adam Weishaupt?'

'Was he the original Batman?' asked Florence.

Blandon shook his head. 'No. He was a Bavarian law professor who founded the Illuminati way back in 1776. He believed that corrupt governments around the world should be replaced with a new global authority. The New World Order.'

Florence gasped.

'In 1784 the Bavarian Elector outlawed secret societies,' continued Blandon. 'Weishaupt went into exile, and the Illuminati died out.'

Florence breathed a sigh of relief.

'Or did it?' asked Blandon.

Florence gasped.

'Yes,' said Blandon.

Florence breathed a sigh of relief.

'Or is that just what they wanted us to think?' asked Blandon.

Florence gasped.

'Yes,' said Blandon.

Florence had been expecting to breathe a sigh of relief, but had to gasp again.

'Weishaupt's secret society lived on,' explained Blandon. 'But this time in extra secrecy.'

'A doubly secret society?' asked Florence.

'That's right,' said Blandon. 'They became so secret they stopped being secret and even printed their all-seeing eye emblem on the one-dollar bill. It was their way of telling us that they were watching us all the time. As well as mocking all the sheeple who remained blind to their power.'

Florence snorted. She hated those sheeple. Why wouldn't they wake up?

'But surely they aren't still trying to achieve their New World Order?' asked Florence.

'Trying?' retorted Blandon. 'They achieved it years ago. They've been behind every government in the world for the last couple of centuries.'

Florence gasped and snorted at the same time, giving herself hiccups.


## Chapter 37

Giuseppe stared at the grid of numbers on his computer screen. He'd been staring at the eighty-one numbers for twenty minutes and they still made no sense to him.

His phone rang.

*Inspector Fascist.*

He let it ring.

The last thing he wanted was that disgruntled old leopard barking at him again. He had no right to talk to him like that. His uncle was the chief of police. Next time Fascist insulted him, he'd go straight to Uncle Despot.

Giuseppe stared at the numbers again. They still made no sense.

Maybe he should give up trying.

Why should he care about these big-shot puzzleologists anyway?

They hadn't let him join their stupid faculty. That's why he'd had to take this dead-end puzzle job. And now they expected him to bust a gut to save their asses?

He remembered his interview with Professor Companion. The renowned grey-haired professor had sat smugly behind his desk, probing him deeply with his eyes.

'Just a few simple questions,' he'd said, lulling him into a false sense of security. 'Before Mount Everest was discovered, what was the highest mountain in the world?'

Giuseppe swallowed back an avalanche of fear. He'd revised anagrams, jigsaws and sliding block puzzles.

*One thing he hadn't been expecting was mountains.*

Miraculously, an answer swooped into his brain.

'K2,' he gasped.

Professor Companion shook his head, a smirk dancing cleverly on his lips.

'Wrong,' he said. 'Mount Everest was still the highest mountain in the world before it had been discovered.'

Giuseppe cringed. Okay, so he'd got it wrong, But surely they wouldn't hold that against him? It was a really hard puzzle.

Professor Companion cocked his head and peered at him. 'If there are six apples and you take away four, how many do you have?'

Giuseppe's heart lifted. He knew this one.

'Two apples,' he shouted. 'If you take four apples away

from six, you get two apples.'

'Wrong,' grinned the professor. 'If *you* take away four apples, *you* have four apples. The four *you* took.'

Giuseppe ground his teeth together and dug his nails into his palms. He tried to grin, desperate not to let the professor know his tricks were getting to him.

'I'm sorry,' he said. 'I meant to say "four". Try another one.'

'Very well,' said Professor Companion. 'If you divide thirty by half and add ten, what do you get?'

Giuseppe ran the question over and over in his mind, checking for hidden traps. There weren't any. It was a simple maths problem.

'Twenty-five,' he said confidently.

'Wrong,' said Professor Companion. 'If you divide thirty by 0.5 you get sixty. Add ten to that and you get seventy.'

Giuseppe's heart plunged.

That was it.

*He'd failed.*

Those three difficult questions had consigned him to life in the purgatory of a police department instead of the paradise of fame, money and women that big-name puzzleologists like Robert Blandon enjoyed.

Why did he have to get questions on mountains, apples and maths? Why not something he actually knew about, like Scrabble, Scattergories or magic squares?

Giuseppe snapped out of his flashback.

*Magic squares.*

That was it.

That's what this puzzle was.

*It was a magic square.*

## Chapter 38

'Why doesn't someone speak out against the Illuminati?' pondered Florence.

'They try,' asserted Blandon. 'But the Illuminati also run the media, and whenever someone tries to expose them they edit the footage to make them look insane. Take the respected British academic David Icke for example. Whenever he appears on television or the Internet, the Illuminati edit his footage to make him sound like a gibbering paranoid lunatic.'

'You're right,' said Florence. 'They do make him sound like that.'

'Another example is the renowned US talk show host Alex Jones,' explained Blandon. 'They've even found a way to apply a filter to his live broadcasts so he sounds like a deluded, sweaty loudmouth undergoing a nervous breakdown.'

'I saw him on CNN's *Piers Morgan Show*,' said Florence. 'They must have turned the filter pretty high that day.'

'I've never explicitly named the Illuminati in any of my works,' said Blandon. 'In case they gave me the same treatment. But I attacked them in acrostic form in Chapter One of my book *Su Doku and the New World Order*.'

'Acrostic?' struggled Florence.

'It's an advanced type of puzzle,' said Blandon. 'The first letter of each line of Chapter One spells out "I'm on to you British Royal family, US government, global banking cabal, Rothschilds, Rockefellers, Merovingians, Jay-Z, Beyoncé, Lady Gaga, Simon Cowell, Tupac Shakur (yes, I know you're not really dead) and that guy who keeps parking outside my house. I know what you're doing. I am not your bitch. The only reason I can't say this more openly is because it might make me look paranoid. But you'll be first against the wall when we rise up".'

Florence played back the chapter in her mind. He was right. The first letters of the lines of the first chapter *did* spell out this message.

Blandon turned to Florence and penetrated her with his eyes. 'Did your father ever write about the Illuminati?'

Florence thought about it. 'I don't think so. Why?'

Blandon's blood ran cold. This was the bit he'd been dreading.

Blandon sighed. 'Because I think it was the Illuminati that killed him.'

## Chapter 39

The assassin leapt off her bike and strode purposefully across the Piazza Santa Trinita.

A man wearing a tweed jacket was waiting by the doorway.

She couldn't believe the arrogance of these fools. They thought they could guide their precious Blandon to safety. Instead, they were sentencing themselves to death.

As if she wouldn't be able to follow their pathetic little trails.

She was awesome at puzzles.

She could walk into a job in any puzzleology department in the world if she wanted. But she'd chosen to use her skills for a higher purpose.

Getting this good at puzzles had been hell.

*A hell she'd gladly volunteered for.*

She had been through nine circles of her hell, just like the ones the great master Dante had described. Each one had torn her soul into pathetic pieces.

*Turning her into the shade.*

Circle One:

Anagrams.

Circle Two:

500-piece jigsaws.

Circle Three:

*Dr Kawashima's Brain Training for Nintendo DS.*

Circle Four:

*Where's Wally?*

Circle Five:

Solitaire.

Circle Six:

Pictionary.

Circle Seven:

Quick crosswords.

Circle Eight:

Cryptic crosswords.

Circle Nine:

Lateral-thinking puzzles.

These last puzzles had been the most punishing of all, but she'd devoted every part of herself to them.

Every morning, the Pathfinder would pose a new, tougher lateral-thinking puzzle and refuse to give her anything to eat or drink until she'd solved it.

'A man walks into a bar and asks for a glass of water,' the Pathfinder had said. 'The barman pulls a gun on him. The man says "Thank you" and leaves. Why?'

Two days and nights she'd sat awake in her cell in the organization's headquarters, trying to come up with the answer.

The Rubik's Snake she wore around her thigh at all times cut into her flesh, but it was nothing compared to the pain the puzzle was inflicting upon her soul.

Then, as if in response to the agony she was subjecting it to, her body gave her the answer.

She hiccupped.

*Of course. The man had the hiccups. He'd wanted a glass of water to cure them, but the barman had shocked him instead, which had the same effect.*

The Pathfinder had been impressed when she'd gone to him with the answer. But his next puzzle had been even more fiendish.

'A man is pushing a car to a hotel. When he gets there,

he knows he's going to be bankrupt. Why?'

She'd gone four days without sleep trying to work this one out. Blood trickled down her thigh as she wound the Rubik's Snake tighter and tighter. She felt as though the fiendish puzzle was imprisoning her.

Then it came to her.

Prison.

*Go directly to jail.*

*Do not pass Go.*

The puzzle was about a man playing Monopoly.

'Very impressive,' said the Pathfinder when she gave him her answer. 'But I wonder if you can tell me what's going on in the following scenario...'

He sat back in his leather chair, resting his chin cleverly on the tips of his fingers.

'A man lives on the twentieth floor of a building,' he began. 'Every day he takes the elevator to the ground floor and goes to work. But when he returns home, he takes the elevator to the tenth floor and walks up ten flights of stairs to his apartment. Why does he do it?'

She had spent a whole week thinking about this problem.

*Obsessing on it.*

A week without food and water. She wound her Rubik's Snake tighter than it had ever gone before, sobbing with pain as the sharp plastic cut into her flesh. She devoured the pain of this ritual. It was her sustenance.

Finally, after a week, hallucinating from lack of food and sleep, she thought she saw a dwarf running outside her window.

When she rubbed her eyes, the dwarf was gone.

But she had her answer.

The man in the puzzle was a *dwarf*.

The Pathfinder had been impressed when she'd told him the answer. No one had ever solved the puzzle in just a week before.

She had journeyed through the ninth circle.

Her trip through hell was over.

Now it was time to help the organization.

To perform her duty to mankind.

*It was time for her inferno.*

## Chapter 40

*Bang.*

The gun barked angrily and Dr Cipher felt heat sear into his stomach.

*My stomach.*

He felt the familiar sting of stomach acid pouring into his chest cavity, and knew he had just seven minutes left to live.

He was meant to help Blandon.

But now he'd be unable to.

Because he had just seven minutes left to live.

Actually, it was more like six now.

He chewed off the end of his finger and began to write in blood on the pavement.

*Bang.*

Dr Cipher felt heat sear into his heart.

*My heart.*

He knew from the throbbing ache in his right ventricle that he now had just two minutes left to live.

Better get on with his message, then.

*Bang.*

He felt heat sear into his brain.

*My brain.*

He knew from the sharp pain in his frontal lobe that he had just five seconds left to live.

*Finish my message.*

Four.

*I must finish my message.*

Three.

*Almost done now.*

Two.

*Finished it. Phew!*

One.

## Chapter 41

Fascist raced across the Piazza Santa Trinita.

He'd thought that little turd Giuseppe had lost his mind when he'd started bleating on about magic squares. Fascist had seen plenty of squares in his life and none of them had been the slightest bit magic.

But apparently it all meant that he had to come here to the Santa Trinita church if he wanted to catch Blandon.

Well, there was no sign of him yet.

It looked like Giuseppe had failed him once again.

Fascist was turning to leave when he noticed something in the shadows at the side of the church's sixteenth-century façade.

A dark figure was dragging something into the light.

*A dead body.*

Wearing a tweed jacket, a black turtleneck and loafers.

Another puzzleologist.

'I've got you now, Blandon,' yelled Fascist, dashing over to the church.

The figure emerged from the shadows.

It was a woman with cropped blonde hair and a black leather motorcycle suit.

'Whoops, sorry,' said Fascist. 'You haven't seen a guy called "Robert Blandon", have you?'

'No,' said the woman. 'I'm afraid I haven't.'

'Well, if you see him, tell him I'm looking for him,' said Fascist.

'Will do,' said the woman. She took a bottle of lighter fluid out of her pocket and began pouring it on the corpse.

Fascist turned and walked away from the woman, his cheeks flushing with embarrassment. This was all Giuseppe's fault. Telling him he'd be able to catch Blandon red-handed, when it turned out there was just this woman here.

Fascist heard a loud whoosh behind him as the woman set the body on fire.

## Chapter 42

Blandon puffed with exhaustion as he arrived at the Santa Trinita church. This night was taking its toll on his athletic academic frame.

Blandon looked up at the church. The current building was constructed in the thirteenth century over a church that had been built there almost 200 years earlier. It contained twenty chapels and several noteworthy frescos.

On the ground beneath the façade was a charred carcass. Blandon wondered if one of the local restaurants had overcooked a pig and tossed it out into the street.

Blandon moved closer.

His heart raced.

His mouth gasped.

There were the charred remains of a pair of cordovan loafers on the pig's trotters.

It wasn't a pig at all.

*It was a puzzleologist.*

He'd been burned.

But he'd left a message on the pavement.

In blood.

Blandon got down on his knees and inspected the message:

QHBZB ROT13

Florence gaped at it. She wondered if it was one of those fancy anagrams Blandon had been talking about earlier.

But how could it be?

There was only one vowel. And there were also two numbers.

Surely even Blandon wouldn't be able to solve an anagram that hard.

When she saw what Blandon did next, she thought she was going crazy.

The Harvard puzzleologist dipped his finger into the blood trickling from his head and began to write on the pavement.

'Now *you're* writing a secret message?' she gasped.

'No,' said Blandon. 'I'm solving one. "ROT 13" stands for "rotate by thirteen places". It's a substitution cipher that replaces a letter with the one thirteen letters along in the alphabet. So to solve it you need to write the first half of the

alphabet above the second half. Like this…'
Blandon pointed to the letters he'd written on the floor.

A  B  C  D  E  F  G  H  I  J  K  L  M
N  O  P  Q  R  S  T  U  V  W  X  Y  Z

Q  H  B  Z  B
D  U  O  M  O

Florence blurted out a loud sigh of amazement at Blandon's puzzle skills.

'The Duomo,' she cried. 'He wants us to go to the Duomo!'

## Chapter 43

The Pathfinder pulled back the hood of his cowl and looked at the pictures in front of him. He smiled. His apprentice had done well.

She'd killed loads of puzzleologists.

And soon the greatest puzzleologist of them all would be dead.

*Robert Blandon.*

And then his gift to the world would be complete.

*His inferno.*

He looked up at the painting of Dante on the wall in front of him.

*Don't be afraid. Our fate cannot be taken from us. It is a gift.*

He liked quoting bits of Dante to himself too.

## Chapter 44

Blandon raced down the street, his wounded head spurting blood along the shop windows.

Florence ran after him. Something was preying on her mind. Another detail of the photograph. She took it from her pocket and glared at it again.

There were two things that looked like large pink socks in the bottom right of the picture.

Florence gasped.

They weren't socks at all. They were her father's small intestines, arranged into a square. He must have pulled them out and placed them like that after he'd split his body open, written the riddle on the floor, daubed the Michelangelo anagram on his calf, traced the rose on his chest, drawn the blood triangle, plucked his eye out and placed it inside. But why?

Blandon turned back to her. 'We need to get to the Duomo.'

'I've noticed something else on the photo of my dead dad,' she said. 'I think you should take a look.'

She held the picture up to Blandon and pointed to the intestines.

'What the hell?' breathed Blandon.

'It's weird, isn't it?' asked Florence. 'Why would my dad arrange his small intestines into the shape of a square?'

'That's not a square,' said Landon. 'That's the square and compasses. The symbol of the deadliest secret society of all. *The Freemasons.*'

## Chapter 45

Blandon's Harvard class on Freemasonry was always packed. He remembered looking out at the eager sea of faces in the Sanders Theater. The creaky old lecture hall was stuffed with thousands of students, many of them dangling down from the building's ancient wooden rafters, holding on desperately with their fingertips for a chance to see the great Blandon in his element.

'What can you tell me about the Freemasons?' asked Blandon.

A wide-eyed athletic freshman threw his hand into the air. 'They're a powerful shadowy organization who secretly run the world.'

A pretty blonde student with gentle blue eyes stuck her hand up. 'They drink blood from human skulls.'

She closed her eyes to reveal the words 'love you' written on her eyelids, like in *Raiders of the Lost Ark*.

An enthusiastic young freshman who was dangling from one of the rafters shouted, 'They worship Satan, except they call him the Great Architect of the Universe.'

'Yeah,' shouted a boisterous young jock in a hockey sweater. 'And they hump goats.'

Laughter thundered around the classroom.

Blandon switched his projector on to show his first PowerPoint slide. It showed a group of elderly men with benign smiles standing in a large hall wearing aprons and drinking cups of coffee.

'Sorry to disappoint you all,' said Blandon. 'But none of this is true.'

A wave of audible disappointment swept around the room. The wide-eyed freshman slumped back in his chair.

The jock rolled his eyes. The kid dangling from the roof loosened his grip and crashed down to the floor. The pretty blonde girl closed her eyes to reveal the words 'that sucks' written on her eyelids.

'The truth of the matter is that the Freemasons are a peaceful organization dedicated to social, moral and intellectual improvement,' said Blandon.

A loud boo echoed around the room and the blonde girl began to sob quietly.

'Some say the roots of the organization can be traced back to the builders of King Solomon's Temple or the Egyptian Pyramids,' explained Blandon. 'But it seems more likely that it has its roots in the stonemasons guilds of the middle ages. Secrecy would have had a practical purpose here, to keep trade knowledge under wraps and protect the profession.'

Blandon switched to his next slide, which showed the first edition of the *Book of Constitutions*.

'Over the next few centuries, Freemasonry developed from trade union to philosophical fraternity. The Grand Lodge of England was formed in 1717, and six years later the *Book of the Constitutions* was published. The society was intended as a haven from the religious divisions of the outside world. This is why they refer to the "Great Architect of the Universe" rather than the Christian God.'

The jock with the hockey shirt let out a loud sigh. He hadn't queued up for five hours to get a front-row seat for this level-headed crap. This was the great Blandon he'd heard so much about?

*Sheesh.*

Blandon switched to the next slide, which showed the inside of a masonic lodge with a chequered floor.

'The organization expanded globally soon afterwards, and an official charter was awarded to St John's Grand Lodge in Boston in 1733. Freemasonry remains a popular pastime to this day, and its lodges are noted for their donations to local causes such as children's hospitals.'

Blandon switch forward to the next slide, which showed the elderly men from the first image again. Except that their genial smiles had been replaced by evil grins, the cups of coffee had been replaced by human skulls full of blood, one of the old guys at the back was having sex with a goat, and Satan himself was standing behind the altar at the back of the room with his hooves gleefully outstretched.

'Just kidding,' said Blandon. 'Everything you've heard about these goat-humping bastards is true.'

A loud cheer rang around the wooden hall. As one, the students got to their feet and chanted 'Blandon! Blandon!' The attractive blonde girl closed her eyes to reveal the message 'love you again' and the jock in the hockey shirt jumped in the air and did a backflip.

*It had been another awesome lecture.*

## Chapter 46

'Why did my father want to remind us of the Freemasons?' asked Florence.

Blandon's blood ran cold. This was the bit he'd been dreading.

'I think they might have killed him,' said Blandon.

'But why?' pleaded Florence.

'He probably revealed one of their secrets,' said Blandon. 'They always kill people who reveal their secrets. They've infiltrated every government in the world, and they're on the verge of overthrowing civilization itself. That's why they're so keen to keep their plans under wraps.'

Florence pointed across the street, to a stone building with a square and compass sign hanging down from it.

'There's a lodge over there,' she said. 'We could pop in and ask them.'

They forced the front door open and barged their way through to a large hall with a chequered floor where a group of elderly men wearing aprons were standing around and sipping coffee.

'Excuse me,' shouted Florence. 'Have you guys been murdering puzzleologists?'

'No,' said one of them.

'Okay,' said Florence. 'Sorry to bother you.'

She walked out of the hall, and Blandon followed her. Just before he left, he turned to address the men, jabbing his finger forcefully in the air.

'And stop humping goats!' he shouted. 'You dirty bastards.'

## Chapter 47

*Bang.*

A painful bullet seared into Dr Tangram's stomach. He staggered across the Piazza del Duomo and fell to the floor. He knew he had just minutes to live. Not enough time to call an ambulance, but enough time to scrawl a puzzle on the floor.

He dipped his finger into his wound and…

*Bang.*

This one got went into his brain and he died.

## Chapter 48

The assassin put her gun back into her holster. The puzzleologist wasn't moving at all now. She should probably have waited for him to scrawl a puzzle on the ground in his own blood like the rest of them.

She shrugged. There was nothing to do but go back to her base and wait. Blandon would figure out where this was all leading eventually. And then she'd complete her mission.

*By killing him.*

It was her gift.

It was her inferno.

## Chapter 49

Blandon stared up at the Basilica di Santa Maria del Fiore, more commonly known as the Duomo, after its famous red-tiled dome.

The Duomo took almost 150 years to complete, and was finally finished in 1436. The original façade was torn down in the sixteenth century and the famous neogothic façade that now stands was designed by Emilio de Fabris in 1871. Inside it, 463 steps lead up to the top of the dome, offering wonderful panoramic views across the city.

Blandon glanced across at the freestanding campanile next to it, also known as Giotto's bell tower. With sides of 14.5m (47.4ft) and a height of 84.7m (277.9ft), the tower houses seven bells ranging from 75cm to 2m in diameter.

Next he looked across at the eleventh-century Battistero di San Giovanni, also known as the Baptistry of Saint John. This unusual octagonal building was clad in white and green marble.

'Why have you stopped to look at these famous tourist sites?' asked Florence. 'We're supposed to be looking for the next puzzleologist.'

'Sorry,' said Blandon. He followed her across the piazza.

Florence let out a gasp.

In front of the cathedral, there was someone lying on the ground.

Blandon ran up to the prone figure.

It was the body of a puzzleologist. His arms were stretched out on either side of him. Wooden stakes had been driven through both wrists. Another wooden stake had been driven through his ankles, just above his Somerset loafers.

A crucifixion.

*To mine eyes there rushed one crucified with three stakes to the ground.*

More words from Dante's *Inferno*, which Blandon had memorized with his massive brain.

Who had done this? And why?

Why?

*Why?*

Why?

'It's Dr Tangram from my father's faculty,' gasped Florence.

She stalked around him, peering at the trickles of blood around his arms and feet. 'Look! He's left a message in his own blood.'

She pointed to his ankles. 'It says... Actually, that's not writing at all. It's just some blood that came out of his ankles.'

'Oh,' said Blandon. 'So he didn't leave any puzzles for us, then?'

'I don't think so,' said Florence.

Blandon and Florence were silent for a moment.

'So… er… what should we do?' asked Blandon.

Florence glanced over her shoulder.

'We could go to the Hard Rock Café if you like,' she said. 'I got a discount voucher last time I went to the Uffizi.'

'All right,' said Blandon.

## Chapter 50

The Florence branch of Hard Rock Café opened in June 2011. It serves a wide selection of appetizers, as well as pizzas, sandwiches and burgers. Not to mention desserts. Rock memorabilia on display in the café includes a bass guitar owned by Flea from the Red Hot Chilli Peppers, a pink shirt worn by Mick Jagger on the Steel Wheels tour and a Vespa scooter used in the Who film *Quadrophenia*.

Blandon sat down at one of the booths and pressed a handful of paper towels against his head wound.

Florence looked at the menu for a moment.

'Are we getting starters?' she gasped.

'I don't mind,' said Blandon. 'It's up to you.'

'I can't decide,' said Florence.

The waitress strode purposefully over to their table like a leopard circling its prey.

'Have you decided yet?' she asked.

Florence felt her pulse quicken. A bead of sweat ran down her forehead. She couldn't work out whether to have the Caesar salad or the club sandwich.

Her heart raced in her mouth as she decided to go for the salad.

Blandon ordered a cheeseburger.

*With Monterey Jack cheese.*

They sat in silence for a couple of minutes.

Blandon pointed to a framed Mötley Crüe gold disc on the wall next to them. The album cover, which was next to the shining disc, showed a pentagram.

'A lot of people associate the symbol of the pentagram with evil,' said Blandon. 'But it's a beautiful and magical symbol for many cultures. The ratios of all the line segments equal phi…'

'Sorry,' said Florence. 'Could we give all this symbol stuff a rest for a few minutes? I'm not being rude. It's just this is the first time I've sat down all night.'

'Fine,' said Blandon.

He listened to the music playing in the background. A track by Northern Irish indie band the Divine Comedy had just finished, and 'Disco Inferno' by the Trammps was starting.

He wondered if these songs were somehow connected to the night's events.

'I should have ordered the club sandwich,' said Florence. 'Do you think it's too late to change?'

'I don't know,' said Blandon.

'Actually, I'm fine with the salad,' said Florence.

A couple of minutes later, the waitress rushed back to their table.

'I'm very sorry,' she said. 'We're out of Monterey Jack cheese.'

'What the hell?' asked Blandon.

## Chapter 51

Fascist rushed across the piazza and anger welled through his body. He was too late, yet again. That useless Giuseppe had taken so long to crack the code that Blandon was probably three or four murders ahead by now.

He'd laid this one out on the floor as if it had been crucified. Fascist circled the body to look for the next code, but there was nothing written there at all.

He plunged his hand into his pocket and grabbed his phone.

'There are no puzzles at all this time,' he said to Giuseppe when the lazy fool had finally picked up. 'Just a body.'

'What does it look like?' asked Giuseppe. 'Maybe the body itself is the clue.'

'It's been laid out on the floor like it's been crucified,' said Fascist.

'Maybe that's the clue,' said Giuseppe. 'Maybe the next puzzleologist is outside a church.'

'Well, that narrows it down,' taunted Fascist. 'I think we had a couple of places matching that description last time I checked.'

'All right,' said Giuseppe. 'I was just trying to help.'

'Well, I don't need any more of your silly guesses,' blasted Fascist. 'I need results. And I don't want to hear from you until you've got them.'

He shoved his phone back in his pocket. Maybe this was all for the best. With idiots like Giuseppe on the case, he was guaranteed to stay a few steps behind Blandon if he followed the trail of clues. He'd have more chance of tracking him down by dashing randomly around the streets.

He decided that's just what he'd do.

## Chapter 52

Blandon finished his burger, wiped his mouth and threw his napkin onto the plate.

'So, should we get back to running around between tourist attractions?' asked Florence.

'I'd like to,' said Blandon. 'But I'm not sure where to go. If only Dr Tangram had finished his puzzle. There weren't any more clues on that picture of your dead dad, were there?'

'I don't think so,' said Florence.

She took the picture out of her pocket and peered at it.

'We've done the riddle,' she said. 'We've done the anagram, we've done the rose, we've done the eye, we've done the cross on his forehead, we've done the entrails.'

'Woah,' said Blandon. 'Back up a minute. There was a cross on his forehead?'

'Yeah,' said Florence. She showed him the picture.

'What the hell?' asked Blandon.

When Florence had mentioned a cross, he'd assumed it would be the Latin cross, the symbol of Christianity. But this cross had four arms of identical length, broadening at the end.

It wasn't a Latin cross at all.

It was the cross pattee.

*The symbol of the Knights Templar.*

'I think your father was trying to tell us something when he drew this symbol,' said Blandon.

Blandon's blood ran cold. This was the bit he'd been dreading.

'I think he was killed by the Knights Templar,' sighed Blandon.

'Who?' asked Florence.

'The Knights Templar,' said Blandon. 'The deadliest secret society in the world.'

Florence gasped.

'They were a band of warrior monks founded in 1118,' began Blandon.

'Hang on a minute,' said Florence. She turned to the waitress, who was walking past. 'Could we get the bill please?' She turned back to Blandon. 'Sorry, go on.'

'They were a band of warrior monks founded in 1118,' Blandon began again. 'They escorted pilgrims to Jerusalem during the crusades. They relied on donations to survive, and soon accumulated vast wealth. Pilgrims began to place their assets in their hands, and they'd safeguard them for a fee, making them an early form of international bank. When Islamic forces...'

The waitress placed the bill on the table. Florence got her purse out and rifled through it.

'Go on,' she said. 'I'm listening.'

'When Islamic forces regained control of Jerusalem in 1239, the order was forced...'

'Ten per cent is okay as a tip, isn't it?' asked Florence.

'It's fine,' said Blandon. 'When Islamic forces regained...'

The waitress came over to collect the money.

'That was lovely, thanks,' said Florence.

'Do you want me to tell you the secret history of the Knights Templar or not?' huffed Blandon.

'Yes,' said Florence. 'Though if you could just run me through the main points, that would be great.'

'Okay,' said Blandon. 'Many of their members were arrested by King Philip the Fair of France on Friday 13

October 1307. Dante criticizes him for it in *The Divine Comedy*, calling him "the new Pilate".

Blandon paused

*There it was again.*

*Dante.*

*The Divine Comedy.*

*Inferno.*

Why had this been on his mind so much tonight?

'Sorry,' said Florence. 'Is this going to end up with us running to another church?'

'Yes,' said Blandon.

'Right,' said Florence. 'In that case I'll go to the toilet now. It's not like I'm desperate for it, but I'll probably need it while we're running around, and it will be much harder to find one then.'

'Fine,' said Blandon.

He waited for her to return and continued with his Knights Templar facts. 'The Grand Master of the order, Jacques de Molay, was burnt at the stake in 1314. Boring old conventional historians believe the order was suppressed, but renowned, scholarly amateur historians have since discovered the truth about them.'

Florence put her wallet back in her inside pocket.

'For a start,' said Blandon. 'They've proved that the entire order was set up to retrieve documents hidden beneath Solomon's Temple. Documents that proved the Merovingian dynasty are the lineal descendants of Jesus Christ and Mary Magdalene.'

'Are you sure you should be saying this?' asked Florence. 'You're not going to end up in court or anything, are you?'

'Nah, it will be fine,' said Blandon.

'They also passed on secret arcane knowledge to the

Freemasons,' continued Blandon. 'And travelled to the New World hundreds of years before Columbus. And guarded the Holy Grail.'

'When you say "Holy Grail", you mean the bloodline of Christ?' asked Florence.

'No, I mean the actual cup,' said Blandon. 'I saw it in a movie. But get this. The real grail wasn't one of the fancy golden cups, but this really crappy old one with loads of dust on.'

'Okay,' said Florence, getting up. 'Should we run to the next church now?'

'Yes,' said Blandon.


## Chapter 53

The church of San Miniato al Monte stands on one of the highest points in Florence, five minutes uphill from the Piazzale Michelangelo. It dates back to the early eleventh century and is one of the Italy's best examples of Romanesque architecture.

Most of the city's great churches were constructed after the official dissolution of the Knights Templar, but Blandon had reason to believe that the order had visited this church. In fact, he'd recently uncovered anagram evidence suggesting they'd buried documents here revealing the ancient secrets of how to turn base metals into gold and how to tell if plumbers are overcharging you.

Blandon ran up the steps to the church and stopped to get his breath back. The entire place was deserted.

Florence ran after him and peered around.

'I can't see any dead puzzleologists,' she said. 'Can you?'

Blandon checked inside a bin, but there were no severed tweed-clad body parts in it.

'I don't get it,' said Blandon. 'I've proved this place has Templar links. Where else could the cross on your dead dad's forehead have been pointing to?'

'Maybe we are at the right place,' said Florence. 'But we got here before the assassin.'

'In that case, wouldn't there be a puzzleologist waiting here?' asked Blandon. 'Whoever this assassin is, they only go to places where puzzleologists are waiting like sitting ducks.'

'That's what I meant,' said Florence. 'This time maybe we're the puzzleologists waiting to be killed. Maybe we're the sitting ducks.'

Blandon heard footsteps behind him. He turned and looked down the steps. There was a shape coming towards him. It was a woman wearing a black motorcycle suit. And she was carrying a gun.

'What the hell?' asked Blandon.


## Chapter 54

Giuseppe stared at the map on the wall of the Florence police department puzzleology unit. He'd marked the locations of all the murders and drawn lines between them, hoping they'd create a pentagram, but all he could see was a random squiggle.

He squinted and tried to convince himself that they looked like one of the alchemical symbols. Mercury? Tin? The symbol for copper turned on its side and stretched a bit?

It was no use. There was no pattern.

Giuseppe sighed. Maybe if he'd been accepted into the university puzzle department he'd be able to spot something here. But his puzzle skills had become rusty since he'd been working for the police.

He used to be able to get really high scores on *Bejeweled*, *Angry Birds* and *Peggle*, but now he could barely play for two minutes without having to thrust his iPad aside. He'd even had to return the last *Professor Layton* game to the shop, as he couldn't complete a single one of the puzzles.

*No matter how many hint coins he used.*

It was no surprise really. He knew the department wasn't going to stretch him the moment he joined. His colleagues Detective Mills and Detective Somerset had been tracing a serial killer who'd been dumping bodies in the town's piazzas.

They'd spent three months working on the theory that the locations of the bodies traced an all-seeing eye across a map of the city, and in the meantime twelve more people had been killed.

It hadn't taken Giuseppe long to work it out. If you jotted down the first letter of every paragraph of Boccaccio's *Decameron*, you got the exact place and date of each murder.

Like all the many art-themed serial killers that plagued cities such as Florence, the *Decameron* killer had wanted to be caught.

But that was back when he was fresh. When his puzzle skills were still sharp.

Since then, he'd caught killers who'd themed their works on the paintings of Botticelli, the films of Dario Argento and the songs of Zucchero. But it had taken him longer and longer every time.

He needed to work out where all these current murders were leading and he needed to do it fast. And maybe if he proved his worth he might be able to leave this dead-end job and get accepted into the university's puzzleology department after all.

He settled down in his chair and picked up the picture of Professor Companion's body. What was he missing?

## Chapter 55

'What is it?' asked Florence.

'There's someone coming towards us,' shouted Blandon. He looked down the stairs and peered into the gloom. Now that he looked at it again, he could see the shape wasn't a woman with a gun at all, but a plastic bag.

'Actually, no there isn't,' he said. 'It's just a plastic bag.'

'Oh,' said Florence. She sat down on the steps. 'Where should we go now, then?'

'Your dad didn't leave any more clues when he died, did he?' asked Blandon.

Florence took the picture out of her pocket and scanned it again.

'No,' she said.

Blandon paced up and down at the top of the stairs. There had to something he was missing.

The rose cross. Clearly the symbol of the Rosicrucians.

The eye in the triangle. That had to stand for the Illuminati.

The square and compass. What else could it be but the Masons?

The red cross pattee. The Knights Templar, obviously.

*The Rosicrucians.*

*The Illuminati.*

*The Freemasons.*

*The Templars.*

All of them the most deadly secret society in the world.

But why did Professor Companion want to point to all of them?

Secret.

Hidden.

Mysterious.

Blandon gasped.

The secret clues all pointed to a bigger, secreter clue.

Professor Companion had been telling them to go to the most famous secret, hidden and mysterious place in Florence. The Vasari Corridor.


## Chapter 56

Giuseppe stared at the picture of Professor Companion's corpse. There had to be something more to it. Another message.

*The Rosicrucians.*

*The Illuminati.*

*The Freemasons.*

*The Templars.*

That was it! The next puzzleologist would be waiting for Blandon on Rosicrucilluminatemplarmason Street.

But where was Rosicrucilluminatemplarmason Street?

Giuseppe had no idea.

He rushed out of his office and dashed down two flights of stairs to the Google department.

The wall of the high tech room was covered in blinking

blue lights, and the air was alive with the chugging of hard drives, modems and circuit boards.

Detective Nerdy, who ran the department, spun round in his chair. He was eating nachos from a huge bag and spilling triangular crumbs down the Hawaiian shirt that covered his bulky frame.

'I need you to check something out for me,' pleaded Giuseppe. 'I need a location for Rosicrucilluminatemplarmason Street.'

Detective Nerdy tutted arrogantly and typed the words into his computer. Giuseppe hated the way the socially unpopular genius acted like everything was such a huge effort. Just because he knew how to use all this fancy Google equipment, he thought it made him special.

Nerdy swivelled round on his chair and picked up his nachos. 'I got nothing,' he said, munching on the corn snack. 'There's no such street.'

'Try typing Rosicrucilluminatemplarmason on its own,' shouted Giuseppe.

Nerdy sighed, typed the word with one salty finger and pressed return. Steam bellowed out of the back of his sophisticated search computer.

'You're making me push her too hard,' he snapped. 'She's never going to find anything anyway.'

'Fine,' said Giuseppe. He wandered back up the stairs, shaking his head. All that expensive technology, and the high-tech boys had drawn a blank.

He swung the door to his office open and sat down on his swivel chair.

The photograph of Professor Companion's corpse was still on his desk.

Giuseppe's heart raced.

There was another message, but it was so simple he'd been unable to see it with his clever brain.

*The Rosicrucians.*

*The Illuminati.*

*The Freemasons.*

*The Templars.*

Secret societies. Professor Companion had been steering them to a secret place. The Vasari Corridor.

Maybe Blandon hadn't worked it out yet.

Maybe he'd cracked the code before Blandon.

Maybe Fascist could get there first and finally catch him.

Giuseppe imagined his face on the cover of *The Puzzleologist*, *The Harvard Review of Puzzles* and *Take a Break's Take a Puzzle* pullout section.

He grabbed his phone and called Fascist.

## Chapter 57

Fascist's phone was ringing. It was that little worm Giuseppe. He stuffed it in his pocket and let it ring.

He didn't need any more advice from that blithering idiot. Not when he could feel how close he was to Blandon. From now on, he was going to rely on instinct.

Fascist heard a noise behind him. He whipped his gun out of its holster and spun round.

It was just a dog.

He heard another noise and spun round again.

It was just a pigeon.

He heard another noise and spun round again.

It was just an old lady cowering in terror and begging him not to shoot her.

Or was it Blandon in disguise?

Maybe he should shoot her just in case.

No. He'd be able to sense when Blandon was near. This wasn't him. Plus, if he were wrong, there would be loads of paperwork.

He put his gun back in his holster and continued down the street.

## Chapter 58

The Vasari Corridor is a long enclosed passageway of almost a kilometre in length that links the Palazzo Vecchio and the Palazzo Pitti, passing through the Uffizi gallery and crossing over the shops on the Ponte Vecchio.

It was commissioned by Cosimo I de'Medici, the Duke of Florence, to allow him to pass between his residence and place of work without having to mix with the public. It was designed by Giorgio Vasari and constructed over five months in 1564.

Blandon rushed through the Boboli Gardens, passing the Buontalenti Grotto. A small door in the wall marked the secret entrance to the corridor. There was no one waiting outside it, but Blandon spotted some shapes chalked on the front of the door.

An eye inside a triangle.

A cross with a rose in the middle.

A Templar cross.

A square and compass.

To the eyes of the ignorant, these would look like nothing more than childish graffiti. But to Blandon's clever eyes, they were proof that he'd come to the right place. Whoever Professor Companion had sent to help him must be waiting inside.

Blandon tried the door.

It was unlocked.

They ventured into the dark corridor.

Blandon could hear nothing but the echoes of his own footsteps. The only light in the place was filtering in through the large windows that looked out across the River Arno.

'There's no one here,' said Blandon. 'We're completely alone.'

Blandon felt his foot strike something. He looked down. In the dim light he could see a pile of dead puzzleologists. All were lying face down on the corridor floor.

'What the hell?' asked Blandon.

'Hell is exactly where they're going,' said a woman's voice from behind them. 'That's why they're crossing the River Acheron.'

Blandon spun round. There was no one behind him.

'Ready are they to pass o'er the river,' said the voice. 'Because celestial justice spurs them on.'

Blandon recognized the words.

They were from Dante's *Inferno*.

'And as a man whom sleep doth seize I fell,' said the voice.

The handle of a pistol whacked into the back of Blandon's head with incredible force.

Everything went dark.

## Chapter 59

Everything was black.

*This is it*, thought Blandon. *I'm dead.*

*The world's greatest puzzleologist has finally been defeated.*

*The streets will be lined with grieving puzzle fans.*

*Elton John will be recording a moving tribute.*

*Good luck next time a psycho leaves a series of themed clues across a popular tourist destination, because I won't be around to help.*

*But if I'm dead, why am I thinking this?*

*Maybe I can wiggle my toes.*

*Yes I can.*

*I'm alive.*

*But where am I?*

*And what the hell?*

## Chapter 60

Blandon's renowned consciousness faded up again.

He wasn't dead. He was trapped in some sort of small black cave.

No, not a cave.

A small black box made out of fibreglass.

He ran his hands down his athletic, scholarly body. He was naked, except for his tweed underpants.

Someone had stripped him and trapped him in this weird coffin. But why?

Flashes of memory burst into his mind like Satan's own PowerPoint presentation.

The chalk symbols on the door to the Vasari Tunnel... The windows looking over the River Arno... The pile of dead puzzleologists on the floor.

This has been Professor Companion's back-up plan. Five puzzleologists from his department had been waiting to ferry him to safety.

Now they'd all been killed. And he was naked and trapped in a glass box. Typical.

For a moment, Blandon felt like he was trapped at the bottom of the well again, accidentally abandoned by his friends, staring up at the circumpunct of the moon and taking hope from its ancient symbology.

Now he was trapped in the darkness again, only this time he had no ancient symbols from which to take comfort.

And this time it had been no accident.

He heard a scream to his left.

*It was Florence's voice.*

He tried to bolt up, but his head crashed into the top of

the box and pain exploded into it.

He tried kicking the bottom of the box with his legs but pain exploded into them as well.

He tried hitting his fists into the side of the box but pain also exploded into them.

He was sick of pain exploding into different parts of his body, so he gave up and lay still.

'Florence?' he shouted. 'Where are you?'

'I'm right next to your box,' she said. 'My arms and legs are bound with rope. There's a weird-smelling liquid down my legs.'

'Well, that's understandable given the circumstances,' said Blandon.

'No, it's not that,' said Florence. 'I think it's petrol.'

Blandon gasped.

Florence had been doused in petrol and he was trapped in a glass box. Who had done this? And what were they planning?

He needed to escape.

And he needed to do it fast.

'Quick!' he shouted. 'Let's use Noetic science.'

## Chapter 61

Blandon thought back to the Noetic science lesson he gave students at Harvard.

He remembered the first time he wandered into the packed lecture hall and addressed the eager-eyed students.

'Today we'll be having a science lesson,' he announced.

The faces of the excited students fell and a groan echoed around the ancient rafters.

Blandon put his hands up. 'Don't worry guys. This isn't one of those boring science lessons where we apply rigorous methodology and standards of evidence. This is a truer, more enlightened approach where we take the language of science and apply it to New Age bullshit.'

Blandon poured a glass of water and placed it on the very edge of his desk.

'I'm going to demonstrate the power of Noetic science right now,' said Blandon. 'Noetic science is a new breakthrough that proves our thoughts and intentions can change the physical world.'

'Like prayer?' asked a Catholic brunette on the front row.

'Exactly like prayer,' said Blandon. 'In fact, maybe prayer and the healing power of shared consciousness that's been proven by Noetic science are one and the same thing. Science and religion aren't so different really.'

A freshman at the back who was halfway through sipping a can of soda spat it all over the row in front in shock.

*Who is this crank?* he thought. *Science and religion are totally different. At least that's what I've always been told. But wait a minute. What if the people who told me this were wrong? Maybe science and religion aren't so different after all.*

Blandon looked at him and smiled. Another mind had been opened to the deep wisdom of cosmic consciousness. It was all part of the day's work.

Blandon pointed to the glass on the table.

'I'd like you all to stare at this glass,' he said. 'And picture it falling off the table.'

The students stared at the glass, sending eager waves of energy from their keen minds.

The glass didn't move.

Blandon sighed. Their shared consciousness wasn't quite strong enough just yet. He often found this with people who were new to Noetic science. He strode past the glass and gave it a quick shove.

The shove combined with the thought power of the students sent the glass crashing to the floor.

A gasp ran through the room.

'And that's just the start of it,' said Blandon. 'Recent cutting-edge experiments have proved that focused thought can change the growth rate of plants, the direction fish swim and the prettiness of ice crystals on a glass of water.'

A freshman wearing glasses at the front of the class put his hand up and Blandon nodded to him.

'If these people have really got scientific proof that thought can affect the physical world, wouldn't they be winning Nobel Prizes instead of running healing workshops in California and flogging badly produced DVDs from their websites?' he asked.

Instead of answering, Blandon walked over to the whiteboard at the back of the room and wrote the words:

*All great truths begin as blasphemies.*

It was a quote from George Bernard Shaw, and one that Blandon used to win lots of arguments.

The freshman stared at it. 'All great truths begin as blasphemies,' he read. 'You mean that all the things we now believe about the world were ridiculed when they were first proposed. Therefore, anything that's ridiculed must be a great truth.'

Blandon nodded.

The freshman smiled with comprehension. He'd answered his own stupid question.

*Another soul saved from ignorance,* thought Blandon. *You can thank me later.*

## Chapter 62

'Use Noetic science,' cried Blandon.

'What the hell is that?' asked Florence.

'There isn't time to explain right now,' said Blandon. 'We just need to focus our minds on opening this box and loosening your ropes.'

'You want me to undo these ropes with my mind?' asked Florence. 'Is this one of those *Star Wars* things?'

'No,' said Blandon. 'It's all been proved with science now. Okay, let's do the ropes first.'

Blandon pictured a thick rope tying a hand to a chair. Then he pictured the rope coming loose.

'Have they gone yet?' asked Blandon.

'Of course not,' said Florence. 'Are you sure you're feeling all right?'

Blandon wasn't feeling all right at all, in fact. His heart was hammering in his ribcage and his breath was short and frightened. Was this the reason his Noetic powers had deserted him?

Blandon heard footsteps outside his glass box. Another female voice spoke.

The same voice that had quoted Dante before.

'If you're thinking of using Noetic science, don't bother,' it said. 'I've Noetic-proofed this entire area.'

*Of course,* thought Blandon. *That's why it isn't working.*

'I'd save your mental energy if you want to escape,' said the woman. 'Because I'm going to run you through a series of puzzles. If you solve them, you can go free. But if you don't, I'll kill you both.'

## Chapter 63

'Time for the first question,' said the woman's voice. 'What does eleven plus two equal?'

*That's easy,* thought Blandon. *Eleven plus two is thirteen. But it can't be that simple, can it?*

Blandon's clever mind raced through the possibilities. Thirteen was a Fibonacci number. It was the date of the arrest of the Knights Templar. It was the number of stripes on the American flag and it featured prominently on the Great Seal.

This was all simple stuff.

Beginner's level puzzleology.

She knew who he was, and she expected something more from him.

*What was it?*

Of course, thought Blandon.

'Twelve plus one,' he yelled.

'Very good,' said the voice. 'It looks as though you might survive a little longer.'

'I don't understand,' said Florence. 'Why not just say "thirteen"? That's what it adds up to, doesn't it?'

'Uh-oh,' jeered the voice. 'I think someone just said "thirteen". Looks like you're going to have to pay the forfeit.'

Blandon heard the swish of a blade followed by a scream of pain.

It was Florence screaming.

'What's going on?' asked Blandon.

'The bitch just cut my arm,' said Florence.

'You need to leave the puzzles to me now,' said Blandon. 'I think they're going to be really difficult ones. We can't risk any wrong answers. Our very lives are at stake.'

'Okay,' said Florence.

'The answer to the last one was "twelve plus one" because it's an anagram of "eleven plus two",' said Blandon. 'It's one of the most famous mathematical anagrams in the whole of puzzleology.'

'Enough of this chit chat,' said the woman's voice. 'It's time for your next question.'

'Sorry,' said Blandon.

He heard footsteps approaching his glass box and flicking a switch. A tiny vent opened in the top of the glass box. Precious air blew down it and Blandon shoved his face up against it.

*An air vent*, thought Blandon. *My reward for getting the question right.*

Water dripped down the vent onto Blandon's nose.

His heart raced.

This wasn't an air vent. *It was a water pipe.* And it wasn't there to reward him for getting questions right. It was there to punish him for getting them wrong.

'It's another anagram question,' said the voice. 'Can you rearrange the words "now lo yonder" to make one word only?'

Blandon considered it. The last one had been a trick, an advanced-level teaser that only experienced puzzleologists could answer. But this one meant nothing to him. He was sure he'd never heard the phrase 'now lo yonder' before.

But the woman had already told him this one was an anagram. So how could it be a trick question?

'Hurry,' said the voice.

Blandon guessed it wasn't a trick question at all. Just a really hard anagram.

He ran through the possibilities with his large mind.

*Now lo yonder.*

Could he make an eleven-letter word out of this phrase?

He didn't know.

There wasn't enough time.

It reminded Blandon of a game show he'd seen on British television once called *Countdown*. Contestants were given a bunch of vowels and consonants and had to make the longest word they could in thirty seconds. A haunting, mocking tune played as the contestants tried desperately to complete their task.

It was that tune that came into Blandon's head now as he tried to make a word from the letters.

Only this time he wouldn't just lose the *Countdown* winners' teapot if he got it wrong.

*He'd lose his life.*

'Out of time,' snapped the voice.

She sent a small blast of water crashing down onto Blandon's face.

'The answer is "no",' said Blandon. 'You can't make one word only from those letters.'

'Wrong,' said the voice. 'Of course you can make "one word only" from "now lo yonder". It's an anagram. I told you that in the question.'

Blandon pounded his fists against the top of the glass box in frustration.

*One word only.*

*Now lo yonder.*

'Don't tell me the great Robert Blandon has been defeated by such a simple puzzle,' said the voice.

'That didn't count,' said Blandon. 'I didn't understand the question. Give me another one.'

'I don't think I will,' said the voice. 'You know, it occurs to me that you can also rearrange the letter of "now lo yonder" in another way.'

Blandon heard the woman turning a tap.

'Drown, looney' said the voice.

Water cascaded onto Blandon's face.


## Chapter 64

Giuseppe peered at his phone. He'd tried calling Fascist twenty times now, and had no response.

Maybe there was a problem with the network.

No. He had five full bars.

Maybe Fascist had managed to track down Blandon of his own accord and was bringing the murderous Harvard puzzleologist back to the station right now.

That didn't sound much like him, though.

It was more likely that he was shouting at pigeons in the middle of some piazza or going on another random shooting spree they'd have to cover up.

Giuseppe scowled with frustration.

This had been his chance to prove to the world that he could solve puzzles as well as the great Robert Blandon.

His chance for puzzleology fame.

A chance that had been wasted by the incompetence of

his colleagues, yet again.

Well, this time he wasn't going to take it.

He grabbed his Beretta 93R single action automatic pistol, shoved it into his holster and dashed out of the room.

If Fascist wouldn't fetch Blandon, he'd just have to do it himself.


## Chapter 65

Blandon wrenched his head to the side and listened as water splattered down next to him.

It was pouring out at a rapid rate.

How long did he have?

Minutes?

Seconds?

'That last question didn't count,' cried Blandon, his feet kicking against the glass. 'Let me try a different one.'

'Okay,' said the voice. 'I'll ask you some more questions. I'll turn the tap off if you get one right.'

Blandon lifted his head, desperately trying to avoid the rising water.

'How many times can you subtract six from thirty-six?' asked the voice.

Blandon tried desperately to ignore his speeding pulse. He needed to concentrate and work out the puzzle.

$36 - 6 - 6 - 6 - 6 - 6 - 6 = 0$

'Six times,' cried Blandon.

'Wrong,' jeered the voice. 'Only once. After that you're taking it away from thirty.'

Blandon punched the side of the box. The water was rising steadily now, soaking his mullet and his tweed underpants.

'Next question,' said the voice. 'What's so delicate that if you say its name out loud, you break it?'

Blandon thought about it. Maybe there was a kind of thin glass you could break with sound waves. But he'd never read about anything like that in *Clever Science* magazine. What the hell could it be?

'I need more time!' shouted Blandon.

'Silence!' shouted the woman's voice.

'But how can I give you the answers if I don't speak?' asked Blandon.

'No,' said the woman. '"Silence" was the answer. It's what you break by saying its name.'

Blandon kicked the inside of the box with frustration, sending a wave of water up to his quivering nostrils.

*Silence.*

It was the sort of puzzle he'd usually be able to solve with no problems at all. But panic was melting his brain in this hellish fibreglass box. The water was rising higher, lapping over his athletic chest.

'Give me the next question!' demanded Blandon.

'All right,' said the voice. 'A plane flying over the Atlantic dumps a hammer and a feather from its cargo hold. They were both dropped at exactly the same time. Which hits the ground first?'

Blandon ran the puzzle through his mind.

*A hammer and a feather.*

These were the objects that astronaut David Scott dropped on the moon during the *Apollo 15* mission. Footage showed him letting go of the hammer and feather and watching them fall at the same rate to prove Galileo's theory of constant acceleration.

Obviously, Blandon knew the whole event had been

faked, and if you squinted really hard you could see the set of *The Brady Bunch* in the background. But what did this have to do with the puzzle? It was set on earth, not the moon.

'The hammer,' said Blandon. 'The hammer hits the ground first.'

'Wrong,' said the voice. 'I said the plane was flying over the Atlantic Ocean. Neither object hits the ground.'

Blandon tried slapping his forehead, but just smacked his hand against the roof of the tiny box.

There were only a few inches of breathing space left in the box now. Blandon shoved his face right up into the tiny gap and filled his athletic Harvard lungs with precious air.

'I need another question,' shouted Blandon. 'I can do this, I swear.'

'Well, well,' said the voice. 'Robert Blandon, the greatest puzzleologist of a generation is begging me for another question. What a pitiful turn of events.'

'Just hurry up,' said Blandon. 'I'm running out of time.'

'Fine,' sighed the voice. 'As I was going to St Ives, I met a man with seven wives; every wife had seven sacks; every sack had seven cats; every cat had seven kits – kits, cats, sacks, wives, how many were going to St Ives?'

Blandon pressed his nose against the top of the box, snorting the oxygen like it was cocaine on a hooker's back. He needed time to think.

*But time was exactly what he didn't have.*

He thought about it, using up all his remaining brain power with the hard sums.

The man had seven wives.

Seven wives

Every wife had seven sacks.

7 x 7 = 49 sacks

Every sack had seven cats.

49 x 7 = 343 cats

Every cat had seven kits.

343 x 7 = 2,401 kits

1 man + 7 wives + 49 sacks + 343 cats + 2,401 kits = 2,801 things.

Add the narrator of the puzzle and you get a total of 2,802 things going to St Ives.

Blandon was about to give this as his answer when the beginning of the puzzle flashed back into his brain.

*As I was going to St Ives.*

Wait.

There was only one person going to St Ives.

*The narrator.*

'One,' gurgled Blandon as the water splashed down his throat. 'There's only one person going to St Ives. The person telling the story.'

Blandon had expected the water to stop, but it kept on flowing into the box.

'What's the problem?' spluttered Blandon. 'I got it right.'

'No, you didn't,' said the voice. 'There were a total of 2,802 things going to St Ives. The narrator overtook them on his way, why was hardly surprising. People walk a lot more slowly when they're carrying hundreds of cats.'

Blandon shoved his lips into the remaining inch of water and shouted, 'Give me another question. I'll get it right this time!'

'I don't think so,' said the voice. 'You've had your chance.'

## Chapter 66

Blandon pushed his head up to the top of the box. There was less than an inch of air left now.

The water seeped into his ears, lips and eyes.

Blandon held his breath as the water edged to the top of the tank.

Then he felt a strange calmness spreading through his body, replacing the panic.

*That's how he knew he was going to die.*

Images flashed through Blandon's mind.

He was a young boy in New England staying in his room on a sunny day to read *American Puzzleologist* magazine. His friends knew how important his puzzle study time was, and had thoughtfully chosen not to invite him outside.

He was trapped in an abandoned well gazing up at the circumpunct moon and hoping rescue would come soon.

He was graduating from Harvard with a 4.0 average, the highest in the history of the puzzleology faculty.

He was kissing the beautiful, intelligent, professional woman Rome Sidekick outside St Peter's Basilica.

He was kissing the beautiful, intelligent, professional woman Paris Tourguide outside the Louvre.

He was kissing the beautiful, intelligent, professional woman Washington Loveinterest outside the Capitol.

He'd had such an exciting and varied life.

And now it was all over.

The box was completely full.

He was going to die.

He'd always wondered what it would be like to die.

*Now he was going to find out.*

Blandon could feel carbon dioxide mounting in his

blood, the atoms of carbon and oxygen scraping against the inside of his skin and stinging his arms.

His instinct told his brain to breathe in. But his brain, which was much cleverer than his instinct, told it to shut up.

A stupid person would have struggled in vain to break the fibreglass box, but Blandon knew better than to waste oxygen on such a pointless endeavour. He just waited helplessly in the cold water, hoping against hope for the kind of contrived *deus ex machina* that usually rescued him in these situations.

Blandon knew he'd soon reach breakpoint, the critical moment when even a really intelligent person could no longer hold their breath. He also knew he was about to experience hypoxia, a condition in which the body is deprived of oxygen supply. Symptoms would include headaches, fatigue, nausea and a strange feeling of elation.

*These were the final moments of his life.*

The greatest puzzleologist of his generation would die as he'd lived. In a state of confusion in a famous tourist location accompanied by a beautiful woman.

His life was ending.

All that puzzle-solving power, all that symbology expertise, all those secret truths hidden from the sheeple by the powers that be, would soon be lost.

Blandon would have cried, but he didn't want to waste any precious energy using his lacrimal glands.

Instead, he lay still, waiting.

*Hoping.*

As he thought about his athletic tweed underpant-clad body lying motionless in a bizarre fibreglass box in a secret part of the Ponte Vecchio, he had a brief glimpse of his insignificance in the universe. Obviously, he was significant compared to other humans. The most significant puzzleologist of a generation, in fact.

*Probably the best since Leonardo Da Vinci.*

But in the context of planets, stars, black holes and stuff, he was insignificant.

Blandon's head pounded.

*He felt tired.*

A wave of sickness washed over him.

*He felt fantastic and ready to party till dawn.*

But that was just the wave of euphoria brought on by the hypoxia, which he'd predicted, and wasn't surprised by.

Now he felt breakpoint approaching.

Soon rational thought would switch off and reflex would take over.

Here it came.

This was it.

Any moment now.

Yep, that's it.

Blandon passed breakpoint and breathed in.

Water swamped into his lungs, burning like acid.

His mouth flopped open and water poured down his throat.

Bright pain shot into his mind and his eyes lolled open.

Rational thought ceased.

*Robert Blandon was dead.*

No, really. He was actually dead this time.

This isn't just a cheap way to make sure you keep turning the pages rather than checking your phone or pottering over to the TV.

He's actually dead.

The rest of this book is just his funeral followed by thirty chapters of his brother-in-law taking his books and clothes to a charity shop.

He's really, truly, actually 100 per cent dead this time.

## Chapter 67

Robert Blandon opened his eyes.

Light scorched through his cornea, lens and vitreous cavity and walloped onto his retina.

It was the blinding light of a billion scorching suns.

No it wasn't. It was the light of a torch held by a man wearing glasses.

Was he God?

No, God wouldn't need glasses. If he were short-sighted, he'd be able to make his eyes better with God power. It was a puzzleologist. *He'd been rescued by a puzzleologist.*

'He's alive,' the man said. 'It's no surprise. He's known as one of the toughest puzzleologists in the game.'

Blandon's eyes adjusted to the gloom and he remembered where he was.

The Vasari Corridor.

'What the hell?' asked Blandon, spewing endless litres of liquid onto the ancient secret corridor.

On the floor next to him were the remains of a black fibreglass box.

Blandon could now see he'd been trapped in a sensory deprivation tank filled with oxygenated perfluorocarbon liquid.

Breathable liquid.

*Oxygenated perfluorocarbon liquid,* he thought to

himself. *Like in that movie,* The Abyss.

Blandon remembered going to see the James Cameron movie at the Harvard multiplex in 1989. He'd chuckled to himself as he'd watched scenes of a diver using breathable liquid. He knew most of the audience would have no idea they were watching real science, or what the precise physiochemical properties of the liquids were. He decided to tell them one by one, and was asked to leave by the ushers.

And now he'd experienced liquid breathing for himself.

*That's why I didn't die,* thought Blandon. *I wasn't drowning. I was breathing liquid. And it's based on actual science, so no one will be able to complain.*


## Chapter 68

Florence stood up and cradled her wounded hand. The woman with short blonde hair and the leather jumpsuit had splashed petrol onto it while Robert had been dying in the black fibreglass box.

She'd taken a lighter out of her pocket and held it over her and then...

What?

A frightened, sweaty swirl of memories ran through her confused mind.

She'd heard Blandon spluttering his dying breath in the tank. She'd seen the flame light up in front of her fear-riddled eyes.

*I'm going to die,* she'd thought.

*This is it now.*

*My dad's dead.*

*All the puzzleologists from his department are dead.*

*Robert Blandon, the greatest puzzleologist of his generation, is also dead.*

*And now I'm going to die too.*

And then her mind turned to more spiritual matters.

*What happens to us after we die?*

Florence had often wondered if there was life after death, and now she was going to find out.

Her mind flitted to a report she'd read in the last issue of *New Puzzleologist* magazine. A series of radical experiments had recently been carried out at the holistic puzzleology institute near San Francisco that had weighed the body-weight of five human volunteers before and after death.

In all cases it was found that the body was much lighter after death, which proved the existence of the human soul. After all, what other explanation could there possibly be for the fact that the bodies weighed less after death?

Some had criticized the scientists for their sloppy methodology. Others had criticized them for beheading five volunteers. But Florence had been convinced.

*There was a soul.*

*There was life after death.*

She'd consoled herself with these scientific facts as she'd prepared for the flames to engulf her.

Right at that very moment, a shot had rung out in the narrow, secret Vasari tunnel.

The naked flame in her blurred vision had cut out and she'd heard the Zippo lighter snapping shut.

She'd blinked tears out of her eyes to see the woman in the leather jumpsuit rushing away down the tunnel.

A young Italian man with glasses had been racing towards her. He was wearing a tweed jacket and khaki pants.

*A puzzleologist?*

Florence had thought the assassin had wiped out her father's entire department.

Who was this guy?

'Who are you?' Florence had asked.

'I'm Giuseppe Petrarch from the Florence police puzzleology department,' said the man, who she'd now known was Giuseppe Petrarch from the Florence police puzzleology department. 'I came here to arrest you for killing all those puzzleologists, but now I've seen who the true killer is.'

'Robert Blandon's in that box full of water,' Florence had said. 'He's probably dead, though.'

Giuseppe had pointed his Beretta 93R single action automatic pistol at the box and shot it five times. The box had shattered, sending water flooding out over the ancient corridor.

Robert Blandon had slid out helplessly and nakedly like a giant mullet-headed baby.

Giuseppe had taken a torch out of his inside pocket and shone it in Blandon's eyes. 'He's alive,' he said. 'It's no surprise. He's known as one of the toughest puzzleologists in the game.'

*Not dead*, thought Florence. *He's not dead.*

*It's probably oxygenated perfluorocarbon liquid*, she thought next, because she'd also read loads of clever science stuff too.

Then Giuseppe had put his torch back in his pocket and untied her.

'What the hell?' Blandon had asked, spewing hundreds of litres of the liquid onto the floor. This is the same 'What the hell?' as the one in the last chapter, by the way. It's just from a different perspective.

Now Florence was cradling her stinging hand and Blandon was waiting patiently for the liquid to stop flowing out of his mouth, nose and ears.

'I think you'd better see this,' said Giuseppe.

He was shining his torch at the wall of the corridor opposite the windows. It was covered with symbols.

## Chapter 69

Blandon staggered to his feet and gazed at the symbols. Liquid was still pouring from his eyes and blurring his vision, but from what he could make out, the wall had been daubed with symbols from every tradition imaginable.

There were the twelve signs of the zodiac, the symbols of every major religion, ancient alchemical symbols, and emblems familiar from masonic tracing boards such as the three candles, the Ashlar and the forty-seventh problem of Euclid.

The multiple meanings of every single one jangled around his liquid-addled clever head. There was Delta, the Greek letter 'D', the mathematical symbol for change, the secret symbol of the New World Order that signified their desire to change the world and pedestrianize every city centre.

There was the emblem of the Priory of Sion, based on the fleur-de-lis. There was a wi-fi symbol, a pentagram, a handicapped toilet sign, a hand-wash only symbol and the symbol of the artist formerly known as the artist formerly known as Prince, who was now called Prince again.

Over and over again, there were the symbols for the Freemasons, the Illuminati, the Rosicrucians and the Templars.

What did it all mean?

*Ordo ab chao*, thought Blandon. *Order from chaos.*

But no order was emerging.

'This isn't a puzzle at all,' said Blandon. 'It's just a massive collection of random symbols.'

'I was worried you'd say that,' said Giuseppe. 'I was hoping it was a really hard puzzle that only you'd be able to work out. But it looks as though it's just a jumble of random symbols.'

He grabbed Blandon's hand and shook it. 'I'm Giuseppe Petrarch, by the way. I work in the puzzleology unit of the police department. I just wanted to say that I'm a huge fan of your work. I loved the way you used album cover clue evidence to prove that all four Beatles died in 1966 and were replaced by the cast of *Leave it to Beaver.*'

Blandon glared at him with his leaking eyes. This wasn't the time for fan worship.

'I guess I'd better leave it until you've solved the puzzle,' said Giuseppe.

'But I don't think there could be a solution to all this,' said Blandon. 'Usually when I'm following a trail of puzzle-based murders, it turns out that one particular group are responsible, like the Illuminati, or the Catholic Church, or the British Royal Family, or the Beliebers. I followed the trail of deadly secret societies here, to a deadly secret place. I was hoping to find out which of those societies was behind it when I got here. Instead I see every symbol imaginable.'

'Maybe that's the point,' said Giuseppe. 'Maybe we're being told that every secret society and conspiracy theory and alternate history are all pointing at the same truth. A sort of grand unified theory of puzzles.'

*A grand unified theory of puzzles*, thought Blandon. Maybe this kid was on to something. For all the amazing secrets he'd revealed in the course of his academic work and crime fighting, he'd always firmly believed there was a deeper truth behind it all, an enlightenment, sensed by his subconscious but out of the reach of even his brain.

Maybe these symbols were pushing him to this moment of epiphany.

Maybe they were…

'I know why these symbols are here,' said Florence, interrupting Blandon's train of thought. 'That woman painted them to distract us if we broke free. She wanted us to do exactly what we're doing now. To try and make sense of this meaningless jumble of symbols while she got away.'

*She's right*, thought Blandon. *There's no order in this chaos. We're wasting our time.*

'Quick,' he said. 'Let's try and catch up with her.'

## Chapter 70

Blandon, Florence and Giuseppe were running along the south bank of the River Arno. Blandon heard the distinctive purr of 999cc inline-4 engine of a BMW S1000RR bike on the other side of the river.

'That's her!' shouted Florence. She pointed over at a woman with cropped blonde hair and a leather jumpsuit tearing down the street on the motorbike.

'We need to catch her!' shouted Blandon.

They ran down to the river and saw a man tying a fishing boat to a wooden mooring.

Giuseppe took his Florence police puzzleology department badge out of his pocket and flashed it at the man.

'We need to take charge of your boat,' he said. 'Florence

police puzzleology department.'

'Okay,' said the man. 'But only if you carry my fox, goose and bag of beans to the other side of the river. You can only take one of them across at a time, though. If left alone together, the fox will eat the goose and the goose will eat the beans.'

'Can't we just take the boat?' pleaded Giuseppe. 'This is an emergency.'

'Sorry,' said the man. 'Those are my conditions.'

'It's all right,' said Blandon. 'We can do this.'

Blandon thought about it.

He stared at the red fox, the grey goose and the cloth bag full of haricot beans. There had to be a way.

He could take the fox over, then the goose, then bring the beans.

But that wouldn't work. The fox would be left alone with the goose. It would eat it.

*Think! Think!*

Take the beans first, then come back for the fox and…

*And find it's already eaten the goose*, thought Blandon in frustration.

He couldn't see an answer. And he was running out of time. The goose honked at him, as if mocking his failure.

'Wait a minute,' said Blandon. 'I think I've got something. Get in the boat.'

Florence and Giuseppe leapt into the boat and grabbed an oar each. Blandon picked up the goose and jumped in.

'Are you sure you're doing this right?' asked Giuseppe. 'If you take the fox over next, it will eat the goose. If the you take the beans over next, they'll get eaten by the goose.'

'Just row,' said Blandon. 'I've got something.'

Giuseppe sighed and started to row.

When they got to the other side, Blandon leapt out,

plonked the goose on the shore and jumped back in.

'Take us back!' he shouted.

Blandon's heart hammered in his chest as the oars pounded on the water of the River Arno. He couldn't afford to get this wrong. But he was sure he was right.

Back on the other shore, Blandon grabbed the fox.

'Really?' spluttered Giuseppe. 'If we leave the fox alone with the goose, it will eat it.'

'Just hurry!' snapped Blandon.

When they got to the other side, Blandon placed the fox down on the bank.

*And picked up the goose to take back to the other side.*

'What the hell are you doing?' hissed Giuseppe. 'We're supposed to be taking these things across. Not bringing them back.'

'Just trust me,' snapped Blandon.

When he got to the other side, Blandon dumped the goose back on the bank of the river.

*Where it had come from in the first place.*

Then they took the beans across, dumped them, and came back for the goose.

Blandon pointed to the fox, goose and beans.

'All safely on the other side,' he said.

Giuseppe's head was spinning.

Florence applauded. The old man on the other side of the river smiled and waved.

'I guess that's why you're the top puzzleologist in the world and I'm not,' said Giuseppe wistfully.

'You can thank me later,' said Blandon. 'Right now, we need to chase after that woman!'

He pointed down the street. The bike was almost fifty feet away now.

## Chapter 71

A motorbike whizzed past Fascist. He peered at the figure perched on it. It wasn't Blandon. Just that woman with short blonde hair he'd spotted killing the puzzleologist before.

But there were three figures rushing down the street towards him.

A woman.

Giuseppe.

*And Blandon!*

Fascist might have known it. That worm Giuseppe had been in league with Blandon all along.

No wonder he'd tried to throw him off the scent with all that nonsense about books. It had been a ruse to get him out the way and leave his precious Blandon free to kill.

Well, he wasn't going to stand for it any more.

He aimed his gun at Blandon and pulled the trigger.

## Chapter 72

Boom.

## Chapter 73

Ow.

## Chapter 74

That really hurt.

## Chapter 75

Detective Nerdy tossed aside his empty nachos packet and opened a box of Twinkies. Steam was still bellowing out of the back of the massive search computer. Why had he let that idiot from the puzzleology department push the machine so hard? Now he'd probably be up all night fixing its circuits.

The blue lights on the wall behind the computer began to blink rapidly on and off. A long, high-pitched beep rang out from the speakers on the server stack. The dot matrix printers began to clack out rows of ones and zeros. The spools of tape on the mainframe spun round rapidly.

The machine was onto something.

'Search result for "Rosicrucilluminatemplarmason" imminent,' said the computer. Then all the machine's frantic activity ceased and it said, 'Access denied.'

Detective Nerdy let his half-eaten Twinkie fall to the floor. Someone was trying to keep him out.

*But why?*

There was only one way to find out.

*With computer hacking.*

He wheeled his chair up to the chunky grey keyboard underneath the monitor and moved his fingers in a blur of motion.

He came up against five different firewalls, but kept on hacking until he got round them.

A progress bar appeared on the screen.

*He was in.*

The bar reached 30 per cent.

Nerdy fished the remains of the Twinkie from the sticky carpet and chewed on it.

The bar reached 70 per cent.

Then suddenly a loud klaxon noise blared out of the speakers and the lights on the wall began to flash red.

The words 'PERMISSION DENIED' flashed on the screen in red type.

*These guys weren't playing around.*

He hunched over his keyboard, hacking with all his strength until thick patches of sweat spread across his Hawaiian shirt.

He'd never seen such powerful encryption before. Who the hell was Giuseppe messing with?

Eventually, the words on the screen changed to 'Access granted' in green type.

Nerdy flopped back in his chair and wiped the sweat off his forehead as the progress bar reappeared.

90 per cent.

95 per cent.

100 per cent.

Words flooded out of the printer.

'The Rosicrucilluminatemplarmasons… also known as the Conspiratorium.'

Nerdy grabbed his phone and began to call Giuseppe.

## Chapter 76

Darkness.

Blandon was in complete darkness.

*Is this it?* he thought. *Am I dying?*

Then he thought, *No. I've just closed my eyes for no reason. Better open them again.*

Blandon opened his eyes and saw Giuseppe lying on the ground, clutching a bullet wound in his chest. Thick red liquid was spreading on the floor underneath him.

*Blood.*

'You need to get away,' whispered Giuseppe. 'Hurry.'

Blandon looked up and saw Fascist hurtling down the street towards them.

'We can't leave you,' said Blandon. 'Not after you saved us from that assassin. Besides, you know we're innocent. Tell your colleague and let's hunt the assassin together.'

'There's no point,' said Giuseppe. 'He's a very dangerous man. He'll shoot you before I get a chance to explain.'

Blandon picked up Giuseppe's hand and squeezed it. A hot tear rolled down his nose and sizzled on the police puzzleologist's dying head.

'You were a good kid,' he said. 'One of the best.'

Giuseppe squeezed his hand. 'While I was working on the case earlier tonight I kept thinking about how many of the murders were based on Dante's *Inferno*,' said Giuseppe. 'Maybe the clues weren't just pointing us towards the Vasari Corridor. Maybe they were guiding us to the Casa di Dante.'

Blandon thought about it.

*Of course.* All the murders he'd seen tonight had mirrored the punishments of the shades in Dante's *Inferno*.

The Casa di Dante museum was where all the clues were leading.

'I'm sure you've probably worked that out already,' wheezed Giuseppe. 'I just thought I'd mention it.'

'Yeah, I did,' said Blandon. 'But thanks for flagging it up.'

Giuseppe's grip loosened on Blandon's hands. His eyes rolled up in their sockets and his mouth lolled open. Blandon pushed his eyelids closed.

*He was dead.*

Blandon leapt to his feet.

The police officer was still running towards them, firing wildly.

Blandon turned to Florence.

'Run!' he shouted. 'We need to get out of here.'

'Where are we going?' asked Florence.

'I just worked it out,' said Blandon. 'We need to get to the Casa di Dante.'


## Chapter 77

Detective Nerdy tried ringing Giuseppe again. This was typical of the puzzleology department. He'd bust a gut getting through all those firewalls and now he couldn't even be bothered answering his phone to find out the search result.

He screwed up the printout and tossed it in the bin.

It was the last time he was going to do any hacking for those ungrateful puzzleologists.

Nerdy fished another Twinkie out of the box, grabbed his copy of *Obnoxious Hacker Monthly* and put his feet up on the desk.

He'd done more than enough for one night.

## Chapter 78

Fascist stopped next to Giuseppe's body and prodded it with his foot. He'd been shot in the heart. Another of Blandon's victims.

It was no less than he deserved for consorting with a dangerous killer. He'd let his love for the renowned puzzleologist get the better of his reason and he'd paid the price.

Well, Fascist didn't have time to arrange for his body to be taken away. He'd worry about that after he'd caught up with Blandon.

Fascist ran down the street, reloading his gun as he went.

A dark shape was moving on the banks of the river.

*Was that Blandon?*

No, it was just a fox eating a goose that was eating some beans.

Fascist unloaded his gun into them.

## Chapter 79

The Casa di Dante lies on the Via Santa Margherita. It was built in 1910 on the foundations of what's thought to be Dante's birthplace. It now houses a museum arranged on three floors, which is themed around his early life in Florence, his exile in 1301, and his enduring legacy.

Blandon ran up to the wooden door and pushed it. It creaked open, even though they were way past opening hours.

Blandon ventured into the dark entrance hall.

'Hello?' he asked. 'Is anyone here?'

There was no reply.

'Are you sure we should going in?' asked Florence. 'What if that woman traps you in a tank again?'

Blandon thought of himself in the sensory deprivation tank, breathing the oxygenated perfluorocarbon liquid.

*Helpless.*

*Hopeless.*

*Hapless.*

He couldn't face that sort of torture again. He'd felt like he was losing his massive mind.

But he had to go on. He had to try and find out who was behind the murders and why they'd been targeting puzzleologists.

He switched the light on.

Just like in the Vasari Corridor, the wall had been daubed with hundreds of symbols. Square and compasses, all-seeing eyes, rose crosses, Templar crosses, fleur-de-lis and hundreds of random symbols drawn from religion, ancient wisdom and everyday signage.

*Ordo ab chao*, thought Blandon. *Order from chaos.*

It was one of the great axioms of puzzleology. There was always a pattern, always a hidden meaning if you looked hard enough and made the right connections.

But once again, this was just a random jumble of stuff, with no more hidden meaning than a bowl of alphabetti spaghetti.

Then a phrase that Giuseppe had used popped into his mind again.

*The grand unified theory of puzzles.*

Maybe the randomness of all this was the point.

Blandon ventured upstairs, beckoning Florence to follow.

## Chapter 80

Fascist watched Blandon's mullet bob behind him as he dashed through the wooden door of the Casa di Dante.

*Now I've got you, you murdering scum*, he thought to himself.

There was no escape from the building.

Blandon and Florence were trapped.

Fascist reloaded his gun and was about to rush in after them when he stopped himself.

*This time I won't be hasty*, he thought. *This time I won't take any chances. This time I'll call for backup.*

## Chapter 81

Blandon and Florence climbed the last few stairs to the top floor of the Casa di Dante. Blandon flicked the light switch.

All around, he could see reproductions of works by Giotto, Raphael, Michelangelo and Doré. But there was no one here.

He'd come to the end of the trail.

'Hello, Robert.'

A woman with short blonde hair wearing a leather biker suit stepped out of the shadows.

She took a gun out of her pocket and pointed it at him. 'So glad you could make it. Now it's time for you to join your colleagues in the inferno.'

'Wait!' shouted Blandon. 'I need to know who you're working for, and why you've been killing all these puzzleologists.'

The woman snarled.

'The Florence University puzzleology department knew too much,' she said. 'Their research took them too far into the realm of secrets.'

Blandon thought about this. It didn't make any sense. How could a third-rate Italian puzzleology department have uncovered something that he, the greatest puzzleologist in the universe, had missed?

'What?' spluttered Blandon. 'What did they know?'

The assassin sighed.

'I suppose I'm going to kill you anyway,' she said. 'So I might as well show you.'

The assassin took a high-tech portable projector out of her pocket and began to beam an image onto the wall of the museum.

'This is just a small part of the footage we're going to share with the world,' said the assassin.

Blandon stared at the blurry scenes unfolding on the wall in front of him.

'What the hell?' he cried.


## Chapter 82

The footage began with robed figures carrying flaming torches up to a giant owl.

Blandon knew the arcane ritual well. It was the Cremation of Care ceremony, held each year at the Bohemian Grove campsite in Monte Rio, California. Every year, the private Bohemian Club, which contained many of the world's most powerful figures, met at the site for two weeks of shadowy occult worship.

Respected academic Alex Jones had secretly infiltrated

the camp and recorded the rituals in the year 2000. He'd revealed the secret Satanic meanings of the secret ceremony, and his profound revelations had been impossible to dismiss as the incoherent ranting of someone with far too much time on their hands.

But why was the assassin showing them this footage?

Blandon had already watched it several times on YouTube. So had anyone who wanted to find out the truth about who was really running the world.

Blandon's pulse quickened as the camera rushed towards the owl.

This was a level of infiltration that no one had ever managed before. Where the hell had this footage come from?

The camera raced further and further until it went inside the giant owl. After a few seconds of darkness, Blandon could make out a man wearing a blindfold. He had a noose around his neck, his left trouser leg was rolled up to the knee and his right sleeve had been ripped away. His shirt was open, revealing his bare chest, which had a large red cross drawn on it.

*A masonic initiate tattooed with a Templar cross.*

The camera spun around shakily to reveal the man was in a large chamber with ornate wooden carvings on the walls. It was moving too fast for Blandon to see clearly, but the carvings seemed to be the same bizarre mix of alchemical, religious and secret symbols he'd seen in the Vasari Corridor and on the bottom floor of this museum.

*Ordo ab chao.*

*The grand unified theory of puzzles.*

The camera swept across a checkerboard floor of black and white tiles before focusing on an altar with a large cross on top of it.

*A wooden cross with a rose carved in the middle.*

The camera moved up to the wall behind the altar, where a large mural had been painted.

An unblinking eye.

Inside a triangle.

Surrounded by the blazing rays of the sun.

*The all-seeing eye.*

The symbol of the Illuminati.

The camera jolted left to show a row of figures wearing long hooded monk's cowls.

*The uniform of the Rosicrucians.*

The camera jolted right to show another row of figures wearing knight's armour and helmets. White surcoats with red crosses covered their armour.

*The uniform of the Knights Templar.*

Blandon could scarcely believe what he was seeing.

Here was proof that the rituals of the Illuminati, the Rosicrucians, the Knights Templar and the Freemasons were being practised inside one of the most notorious destinations on earth.

*This is dynamite*, thought Blandon. *If this footage is ever released, it will send shockwaves around the world.*

But what he saw next made his jaw drop right open.

The Rosicrucians and Knights Templar crowded around the initiate and attacked him with Masonic gavels and stone mauls.

As the initiate writhed around, spurting dark blood all over the tiled floor, a voice from behind one of the Knights Templar helmets boomed, 'Is there no help for the widow's son?'

'No, there isn't', chanted the others.

Blandon chuckled to himself while the disturbing scene played out. Most people who saw this footage wouldn't realize that the 'widow's son' in question was Hiram Abiff, one of the builders of the Temple of Solomon in Jerusalem. He'd been murdered by three other workers when he'd refused to raise them to the rank of Master Mason. His last words had been: 'Is there no help for the widow's son?' Words that were still used in the murderous rituals of Freemasonry today.

A cut in the bloodcurdling footage and the camera zoomed in on a skull.

*A human skull. Full of blood.*

Was this the skull of the man who'd just been murdered? Blandon shuddered at the notion.

It was too horrible to contemplate.

The skull was in the hands of the first monk. He pulled his cowl back to drink from it.

Blandon's heart raced. He recognized the man's face. He was the leader of one of the most powerful nations on earth. He wiped the blood from his lips and grinned.

One of the world's most powerful men. Revelling in the squalor of an ancient, evil ritual.

One by one, the figures pulled back their hoods and removed their helmets to reveal their identities.

World leaders.

Movie stars.

Prime-time news anchors.

Rock stars.

Hip hop stars.

Sports personalities.

All of them sipping human blood and grinning.

Another cut in the footage and the camera zoomed back to reveal its most hideous sight yet.

*They were all humping goats.*

Dread swirled loudly in Blandon's soul.

## Chapter 83

The Florence Police Department UH-60 helicopter hovered into the courtyard outside the Casa di Dante.

The pilot leaned out and glanced at Fascist, who pointed at the Casa di Dante.

'You can't mean that place,' he said.

'Yeah,' said Fascist. 'Level it. Hit it so hard that there can be no possibility of any survivors.'

'But surely that must be a protected building,' said the pilot. 'Isn't it the birthplace of Dante Alighieri?'

Fascist bristled. He'd heard more than enough about know-it-all writers for one day. So what if it was Dante's birthplace?

*All the more reason to blow it to smithereens.*

'Are you questioning my orders?' asked Fascist.

'No, sir,' said the pilot.

*Good*, thought Fascist. *Because it's time to give that murdering Blandon a taste of his own medicine.*

## Chapter 84

'That's horrible,' said Florence. 'Where did you get that footage?'

'We have our sources,' said the assassin, putting the projector back in her pocket. 'But they're not your concern. All you need to know is that we'll soon be sharing that footage with the world. And nothing will be the same again.'

*No kidding*, thought Blandon to himself.

The assassin raised her gun again.

'But I don't get it,' said Blandon. 'If the aim of your

organization is to share this material with the world, why are you killing puzzleologists? We dedicate our lives to uncovering these secret truths. We're on your side.'

Anger and hatred swirled around the woman's eyes.

'You know nothing of my side,' she hissed. 'That footage is just the tip of the iceberg. Those dead puzzleologists saw too much of the rest of the iceberg, and they had to pay the price. Just like you're going to do right now.'

She pointed her gun at Blandon and pulled the trigger.

## Chapter 85

Boom.

## Chapter 86

Blandon opened his eyes. He was looking out across a river of blood at a pile of corpses who were writhing in pain, clawing and gnashing at each other.

It was just like his dream in the hospital.

Except that this time he knew he wasn't dreaming.

*This is it*, he thought. *I'm dead.*

*And judging by the company I'm keeping, I don't think they've sent me to the place upstairs.*

Blandon couldn't understand it. All his life he'd brought joy and hope to millions of puzzle fans all around the world. Surely he didn't deserve to end up in hell?

*What the hell?* he thought, and chuckled to himself. It was hard to deny the irony of his catchphrase now he'd been sentenced to eternal damnation.

## Chapter 87

Fascist grinned to himself as he watched the three-storey building collapse into rubble.

On his command, the helicopter had used its 2.75in rocket launcher to fire a Mk 40 Folding Fin Aerial Rocket into the ground floor of the Casa di Dante. The building had collapsed with an almighty boom, sending plumes of smoke out into the sky.

He jumped into the helicopter and the pilot lifted off, banking to the west as clouds of acrid dust filled the narrow medieval alleyways.

Fascist knew he'd have a hell of a lot of paperwork in the morning, but it had been worth it.

*Robert Blandon was dead.*

The world was a safer place.

He'd sleep with a clear conscience tonight, even if it had meant blowing up some old building or other.

## Chapter 88

Blandon stared at the writhing bodies. For writhing bodies, they weren't doing much writhing. They were completely still, in fact.

A bright light shot into his field of vision. A blinding whiteness flashed across everything.

*Is this heaven?* thought Blandon.

It would make a lot of sense. Whoever the spiritual bigwigs in charge of the afterlife were, they'd recognized their mistake in consigning Blandon to Hades and decided to elevate him to paradise.

'There you are,' said a voice. 'I've been looking for ages.'

It was a woman's voice.

*Florence's voice.*

Blandon wasn't dead at all.

He was lying underneath a pile of rubble.

The assassin's bullet had somehow levelled the entire house and he'd been trapped under a collapsed wall with a Gustave Doré print filling his entire field of vision.

Florence had just found him by shining a bright light in his eyes. The light of the portable projector.

He felt Florence grab his mullet and pull him down into a narrow open space. He got to his feet and wiped the dust off his tweed jacket.

'Are you okay?' asked Florence.

Blandon nodded. 'That woman must have one hell of a powerful gun, though.'

'It was a rocket fired by a police helicopter,' said Florence. 'I saw it as it crashed through the wall.'

She pointed the projector ahead of them. It cast images of famous people humping goats on two walls that stretched out ahead of them, the only way out of the pile of rubble in which they were trapped. They were in a narrow tunnel, a secret passageway that had been revealed in the blast.

Blandon noticed chalk markings on the walls.

The square and compass.

The all-seeing eye.

The Templar cross.

The rose cross.

The fleur-de-lis.

The circumpunct.

The Ouroboros.

Sigma.

Delta.

Pi.

'Another jumble of symbols without order,' said Blandon. 'I've still no idea what they mean.'

'They mean we must be going the right way,' said Florence.

She grabbed his arm and pulled him down the passageway.


## Chapter 89

*My gift is complete*, thought the assassin. *My inferno is finished.*

Heavy bricks were crushing her chest. Life was draining from her body. Her breath grew shorter and shorter.

She knew these were the final seconds of her life, but she didn't care. She'd completed her task. She killed all the puzzleologists. She'd kept the secret safe. And as her final action, she'd rid the world of Robert Blandon. Now the loose ends were tied up. The trail was dead. No one alive could possibly uncover the secret now.

'That one's called the ouroboros,' said a voice from below her. 'The symbol of a snake swallowing its own tail can be traced back to ancient Egypt and Greece. It's associated with cycles of rebirth and renewal.'

It was Robert Blandon's voice.

He was still alive.

And he was still wanging on about symbols.

*I have failed*, she thought as her final breath left her body and she died.

## Chapter 90

Blandon strode ahead in the flickering light, snatching cobwebs aside. The sides of the passage crumbled as he brushed them.

He followed the passage around to the right. Even hundreds of feet along it, the walls were still covered with a chaotic mess of symbols.

'Look,' said Florence. 'The tunnel ends there.'

Blandon ducked aside and let the projector cast its light ahead of them.

The tunnel came to a dead end.

*They were trapped.*

Blandon's heart thumped inside his sweater as he tried to stop himself remembering the time he was accidentally abandoned in the well.

He rushed to the dead end and slammed his fists into the walls all around him. They were completely solid.

In desperation, he whacked the ceiling above him.

Loose soil fell into his eyes, his turtleneck and his mullet.

As Blandon crouched forward and tried to blink out the soil, Florence shouted, 'Look! It's a way out.'

Blandon looked up. An ancient wooden trapdoor with a rusty metal handle was directly above them.

He pulled the handle and the door flopped loosely down.

Florence stepped over and shined the projector through the door. There was a small space above them with a flat stone ceiling.

Blandon winced.

*Another enclosed space.*

But at least it might lead somewhere. And that would be better than staying in the tunnel.

Blandon pulled himself up using his athletic arms. He crawled out onto a cold stone floor.

He tried to stand up, but his head slammed into the stone ceiling.

What the hell was this room?

It was as small and quiet as a tomb.

He felt around the space, trying to find a door, but there was nothing.

Blandon thrust his hands against the ceiling.

A long slat of flickering light appeared.

He pushed it with all his strength now, creating a gap he could just about squeeze through.

'It's a way out,' shouted Blandon. 'But it's pretty narrow.'

The Harvard puzzleologist forced his way through, ignoring the pain as the heavy stone scraped his back.

He emerged on the cold marble floor of a building lit by candles.

He stood up, arched his back and looked back to the space he'd crawled out of.

No wonder it had felt like he'd been in a tomb.

He *had* been in a tomb.

*The empty tomb of Dante Alighieri.*

He was in the Basilica di Santa Croce.

He heard footsteps walking down the aisle.

'Robert Blandon?' asked a fruity British baritone. 'Fancy seeing you here.'

## Chapter 91

The man hobbled towards Blandon.

Blandon recognized the mischievous gait. The noble and aristocratic creaking of the metal crutches on his legs. The precise linen shirt, red silk cravat and tweed suit.

This was an old, trusted friend of his.

Sir Lee Teabagging. One of the richest and most eccentric puzzleology patrons in the world.

Blandon knew he kept a town house here in Florence, but he had no idea he was planning to be in the city. He'd almost certainly have arranged to pop round for tea if he'd known.

*Earl Grey tea.*

*With a slice of lemon.*

Red-faced and dignified, with twinkly blue eyes, Blandon had always thought Teabagging resembled the actor Sir Ian McKellen. Or Sir Patrick Stewart if... What? McKellen wants to do it? Are you sure? And he's read the script and everything? Well, it's his decision, I suppose. Blandon had always thought Teabagging looked exactly like the actor Sir Ian McKellen.

'Well, my dear boy,' said Teabagging. 'Aren't you going to let your little lady friend out of her cage?'

He pointed to the tomb.

Blandon chuckled to himself. In his excitement at seeing his old puzzleology friend, he'd forgotten all about Florence, who was banging on the inside of the tomb and screaming.

## Chapter 92

'Oh yes, I approve of this one,' said Teabagging as Blandon pulled the terrified Florence out of the tomb.

'Where are we?' asked Florence. 'And who the hell is this guy?'

'We're in the Basilica di Santa Croce,' said Blandon. 'And this is Sir Lee Teabagging, one of the world's foremost puzzleology patrons.'

Florence curtseyed with regret. 'I'm sorry,' she said. 'I had no idea you were a knight of the realm.'

'That's quite all right,' said Teabagging. 'I'd expect no less from one of Robert's Harvard friends. That was my fifth choice of educational institute when I was applying to Oxbridge, you know.'

Teabagging raised an eyebrow, but Blandon refused to be drawn by it. Sure, England was once the centre of the world for puzzleology studies. It had been home to some of the most prominent puzzleologists the world had ever known.

Sir Christopher Wren.

Sir Isaac Newton.

Sir William Shakespeare.

But now the country's puzzleology scene was little more than a coterie of old pantomime dames bickering about the past.

America was where it was at now.

But if Blandon said that to Teabagging, he'd never hear the last of it.

'Actually, I studied here in Florence,' said Florence. 'I got a double first in puzzleology and gender studies.'

Teabagging raised his other eyebrow.

Blandon willed him not to go there.

'Well, I suppose it must have given you something to do between cooking pasta and attending bunga bunga parties,' said Teabagging.

*Uh-oh*, thought Blandon. *He went there.*

He could see Florence was beginning to smart, so he decided to change the subject.

'What are you doing here?' asked Blandon. 'Did Professor Companion send you?'

'Who?' asked Teabagging. 'Oh, you mean that chap who died tonight? Can't say I've ever met him, darling.'

'That chap who died was my father,' said Florence. 'And he happened to be the most respected puzzleologist in the country.'

'I'm very sorry for your loss,' said Teabagging, momentarily taking off his tweed hat. 'But I'm afraid the trail I followed here had nothing to do with a Professor Companion and everything to do with these.'

Sir Teabagging fished three tiny scrolls out of his pocket.

'What the hell are they?' asked Blandon.

'It's a long story,' said Teabagging. 'And one that calls for the appropriate refreshment.'

He snapped his fingers and shouted, 'Butterfield!'

A butler wearing a black suit and white bow tie wheeled a tea trolley down the aisle of the church. He poured out three cups of Earl Grey and popped a fresh slice of lemon into each one.

'Excellent, Butterfield,' said Teabagging. 'You've exceeded yourself again.'

He turned to Blandon. 'So where were we? Ah, that's right. I was about to tell you all about the quest this particular knight has been on.'

## Chapter 93

'As you know, Robert, in recent years I've devoted much of my considerable resources to proving that the Pyramids of Egypt were in fact built by ancient peoples from the lost continent of Atlantis,' began Teabagging.

'I have good reason to believe that one of the builders of the Pyramid of Khufu accidentally left his return boat ticket between two of the stones on the east side, so naturally I flew my archaeological team over to Egypt and watched them working away while Butterfield fanned me and served tea.

'After four days, the three strapping young men who make up my team had drawn a blank and I started to wonder if the whole Atlantis thing was so much woo.

'Don't judge me for this, Robert. The heat was getting to me, and I was beginning to lose faith.

'Anyway, you can imagine my delight when a spunky little brunette from my crew called Matthew handed me a tiny papyrus scroll he'd found wedged between two of the pyramid's stones.

'I unfurled it with shaking hands. Had I finally found evidence of the beautiful lost race of Atlanteans? Alas, no. But what I found was just as intriguing. On one side of the scroll were the symbols of the Freemasons, the Rosicrucians, the Illuminati and the Knights Templar. On the other side were the words, "Pope's stone? We know nothing."

'Now I doubt this one would have taxed you very much, dear Robert. But I have to admit it took my old Oxbridge brain more than just a couple of sips of Earl Grey to get to grips with.

'You see, my problem was that I'd been looking too much to the old world for the answer, while the real solution lay in your own adolescent little nation.

'As I'm sure you'll have spotted by now, the "Pope's stone" didn't refer to any building in Rome, but a stone donated to the builders of the Washington monument by Pope Pius IX in the early 1850s. This gift angered the Know-Nothings, a political group opposed to Irish Catholic immigration, so they stole the stone from the monument, and dumped it in the Potomac River.

'As soon as I'd established this, I ordered Butterfield to fire up the jet and take us to the capital of your vulgar land.

'Once again, I sent my eager boys up to the top of the erection while I sat on a deckchair below, sipping freshly brewed tea. This time my lads came through for me right away. A scrap found wedged into a window frame in the viewing gallery was transported down the structure on their lithe legs and soon I found myself clutching another miniscule scroll.

'Again, one side of the paper was covered in the symbols of those four secret societies, while a further clue was written on the reverse. If you don't mind me saying, Robert, I think this one would have given even you pause for thought. For this time, the other side of the scroll contained nothing but an equals sign.

'I let Butterfield and the boys go out on the town while I stayed behind in our hotel room, staring in desperation at the enigmatic slip. As far as I could work out, an equals sign could refer to hundreds of places around the world, maybe thousands.

'I was despondent, and refused all my medical treatments

for two days. Towards the end I was even throwing cups of Earl Grey in Butterfield's face. I was in a black mood, that's for sure. But my spirits soon lifted when I held the unfurled scroll up to the window one morning. I found that the light made the symbols on the other side of the scroll show through in such a way that the equals sign fell between the square and compass and the Templar Cross.

'I threw my hands up in the air, dashing tea all over our expensive suite at the Ritz-Carlton. But I cared not. As I'm sure you'll have deduced, dear Robert, the equals sign was pointing me to the one place in the world that proves the Freemasons were the direct descendants of the Knights Templar.

'I'm referring, of course, to the Rosslyn Chapel in Scotland.

'Before the day was out, we were back in the jet and heading for the uncouth country that lies directly to the north of my beloved homeland. By the time we arrived, official visiting hours were over, but a wad of crisp fifty-pound notes was enough to convince the Scotch layabouts in charge to let us pay a private visit to the exquisite site.

'By the next morning, we'd discovered our final clue tucked inside a burial vault deep below the esteemed chapel. Once again, the secret symbols and once again the clue on the reverse.

'This one read, "Inside the Santa Croce, where I do not lie." So I followed the clue here, and here I've been waiting all night.'

## Chapter 94

Blandon shook his head when Teabagging had finished speaking. He could scarcely believe the story the twinkly old goat had told him, yet he knew it must be the truth.

'So why did they send you here?' asked Blandon. 'Why was this the final stop on the treasure hunt?'

Teabagging's wrinkly twinkly face fell.

'I was rather hoping you might be able to tell me, old boy,' he said. 'I got my boys to have a good old rummage around inside the tomb earlier tonight. They found nothing, and since then I've been hoping for someone to come and enlighten me. When I saw your lovely face emerge from the poet's intended resting place a few moments ago I assumed you'd be able to shed some light on the mystery.'

Blandon handed his empty teacup to Butterfield, who wheeled his trolley dutifully back down the aisle.

'I wish I could,' said Blandon. 'Sadly, all I can tell you is that we've also followed a trail of symbols here. Not just the symbols of the Freemasons, Rosicrucians, Templars and Illuminati, but hundreds of others, slapped on walls with no apparent order.'

'This is big,' said Teabagging. 'In fact, I'm sure it's the biggest thing either of us has ever been involved in. But where are we to look now? I'm sure this can't be the end of the trail.'

Florence wandered over to the empty tomb, repeating the clue to herself: 'Inside the Santa Croce, where I do not lie.'

She turned to Blandon. 'What did Dante have to say on the subject of people who didn't tell the truth?'

'Falsifiers got a pretty rough time,' said Blandon. 'They ended up tearing each other apart in the eighth circle.'

'So you're saying Dante would have considered himself a

truthful person?' asked Florence.

'Of course,' said Blandon.

Florence leapt up onto the statue of Dante that sat on top of his empty tomb.

Teabagging leapt to his feet. 'What on earth are you playing at?' he cried.

Florence fondled the stone face of the poet until finally she said, 'Got it.'

She grabbed the statue's right ear and twisted it sideways.

Blandon couldn't believe what he was seeing. The stone jaw of the ancient statue dropped slowly down.

*Dante was opening his mouth.*

'What the hell?' asked Blandon.

## Chapter 95

'Oh, she's good,' said Teabagging. 'You've got a good one here.'

'But I don't understand,' began Blandon.

'The place where I do not lie,' said Teabagging. 'This didn't just refer to Dante's tomb. It referred to his mouth.'

Blandon's head was spinning.

*Of course*, he thought. *The place where I do not lie.*

Florence reached into the poetic stone mouth.

'There's something inside here,' she said. 'If I can just get to it.'

Very carefully, Florence pulled a colourful stone object out from inside the statue.

*It was a cube.*

Each of the six faces had been split into nine smaller squares, painted blue, red, green, yellow, orange and white, seemingly at random.

Florence swallowed her incomprehension and said, 'A Rubik's Cube?'

'No,' said Robert Blandon, stalking purposefully towards her. 'A Da Vinci Cube.'

## Chapter 96

'We did these in college,' said Florence, striding back over to Blandon. 'They were invented by a Hungarian guy called Erno Rubik in 1974. He sold the licence to a toy manufacturer in 1980, creating a pop culture phenomenon that would come to define the decade along with Pac-Man, fluorescent legwarmers and getting so coked up you believe you can fly and jumping out the window of your luxury penthouse apartment.'

'Sure,' said Blandon. 'That's what they tell you in the undergraduate puzzleology course. But when you do the PhD, they let you in on the real truth. The item we now know as the Rubik's Cube was designed by Leonardo da Vinci in 1518, along with a host of other genius inventions that were kept secret until the time of greatest need.'

'Whose greatest need?' asked Florence.

'I believe I can take up the story,' said Teabagging. 'Have you ever heard of the Priory of Sion?'

'Wasn't that a hoax created by Pierre Plantard to convince everyone he was the "great monarch" referred to in the prophecies of Nostradamus?'

'My dear girl, what on earth do they teach you in puzzleology college these days?' gasped Teabagging. He grabbed a red silk handkerchief from his jacket pocket and dabbed sweat from his forehead.

'Forgive her,' said Blandon. 'She's green.'

'I'm only telling you what I've been told,' said Florence, offended.

'Well, try thinking for yourself for once,' snapped Teabagging. 'If the Priory of Sion is really a hoax, why have millions of people bought paperbacks about it? Are they gullible idiots?'

Teabagging wiped his forehead again. The angry sweat was pouring thick and fast now.

'My dear child,' said Teabagging. 'The Priory of Sion is no hoax. It is an ancient organization dedicated to protecting the secret of Christ's living descendants. Past presidents of the society have included such luminaries as Victor Hugo, Claude Debussy, Jean Cocteau and Leonardo da Vinci.'

Florence gasped.

'In 1518, Da Vinci bequeathed a number of inventions to the society for them to release if they ever needed the funds,' continued Teabagging. 'You might know them as the hula hoop, the Rubik's Cube, Hungry Hungry Hippos and the PlayStation 3, but to us properly educated puzzleologists, they're known as Da Vinci's secret gifts.'

'The world hasn't seen all them yet,' said Blandon. 'Wait until you get a load of the time domino and the n-dimensional puzzle vortex.'

Florence handed Blandon the cube. 'So did the Priory of Sion leave this stone cube inside Dante's mouth?'

Blandon furrowed his brow. 'They must have done, I guess.'

'It's certainly a rum state of affairs,' said Teabagging. 'I can't say I've ever come across anything like it before.'

'Me either,' said Blandon.

'Well, it looks like there's only one way we're going to get to the bottom of all this,' said Teabagging.

'What's that?' asked Blandon.

Teabagging pointed at the stone cube.

'Solve the puzzle, my dear boy,' said Teabagging. 'All Da Vinci Cubes were constructed to contain secret messages. And the only way to open them is to solve the puzzle.'

## Chapter 97

Blandon's blood pumped loudly in his ears as he stared down at the multi-coloured stone cube. He'd solved these sorts of puzzles before, of course. But never against the clock. And never with people watching him.

He was going to have to bring his 'A' game.

He'd have to twist the sides of the puzzle around until the small squares on each side of the cube were exactly the same colour.

The problem was, the colours were really mixed up.

Blandon twisted the right side clockwise. A bead of sweat dripped from his forehead onto the ancient stone cube. He told himself to stop. He didn't want the others to sense his fear.

*He didn't want the cube to sense it.*

He twisted the front anticlockwise.

He twisted the left side clockwise.

It wasn't working. The colours were still jumbled up.

*Focus*, Blandon told himself. *It doesn't matter if you don't solve the puzzle right away. You'll still be the greatest puzzleologist of your generation. Not your words, but the words of* New Puzzleologist *magazine.*

But the more Blandon twisted the cube, the more it seemed to get mixed up.

He was a young boy again, trapped down a well.

*Abandoned.*

He tried to focus and complete one side at a time. But it just made the others jumble up more. What use was one completed side anyway? He'd only have to mess it up again to do the others.

Blandon told himself to relax and think back to his seminars with puzzleology grad students. He must have gone through all this a thousand times. Why was it such a trial now?

Focus on the centre piece, he would tell his students if they were struggling. The centre piece can't move, so that's already one square in the right place.

Next, look for the four squares that make up the cross around that centre piece, then worry about the four squares in the corner.

*But it was no use.*

Blandon tried following his own advice, but it wasn't working.

The colours seemed to goad him with their very randomness.

*He couldn't take it any more.*

He needed to teach them a lesson.

Blandon dashed the stone cube down to the floor, and it smashed into twenty-six tiny stone pieces.

As one, Florence and Teabagging gasped.

## Chapter 98

Blandon looked down at the floor, his face red with frustration. A tiny scroll was visible among the pieces of stone.

Blandon sifted it out and held it up.

Teabagging applauded loudly.

'Bravo, dear boy,' he said. 'For a moment there, I thought the facile little puzzle had actually beaten you and you'd walloped it on the floor in frustration.'

'Of course not,' said Blandon. 'I actually used math to prove it was an impossible puzzle, and therefore the only solution was to break it.'

Florence nodded in comprehension.

'So,' said Teabagging. 'It looks like the game is afoot once more.'

Blandon bent down and picked up the scroll. Once again, it had the secret society symbols on one side and a clue on the other.

Blandon unravelled it.

His heart sank.

The clue was complete gibberish.

*sevihcrA terceS nacitaV*

'Well, boy,' said Teabagging. 'What's wrong with you? Read it out.'

'I'm not sure I know how to,' said Blandon.

He attempted to read the strange words.

Teabagging harrumphed.

'Hebrew?' he asked. 'Aramaic? Phoenician? French?'

'That's what I thought,' said Blandon. 'But I can speak

every language ever because I'm so smart, but even I don't recognize any of these words.'

'Then it looks like our revels have ended,' said Teabagging, the twinkle disappearing from his eyes.

'I can read it,' said Florence.

'Don't be so ridiculous!' sputtered Teabagging. 'It's gibberish.'

'Not gibberish,' whispered Florence. 'English!'

'You're babbling, woman,' shouted Teabagging. 'How can those words be English?'

'Because they're written backwards,' said Florence. 'My father taught me backwards writing when I was just six years old.'

Blandon's head spun all the way round.

*Of course.*

*How could he have missed it?*

How many times had Blandon taught his eager Harvard students about backwards writing?

He loved to start the lesson by writing 'treboR' on the white board and telling the students that it was his name. He'd then watch their puzzlement turn to awe and wonder when he pointed out that 'treboR' was nothing more than 'Robert' written backwards.

Backwards writing had been used countless times throughout history to keep secrets safe from prying eyes. The Templars had used it to keep the many locations of their treasure hoards secret. The Illuminati had used it to cover up their role in the promotion of genetically modified crops. And the Nazis had even tried using it until Winston Churchill himself had cracked the code following a three-day Scotch bender.

'I need a pen and piece of paper,' yelled Robert.

Teabagging snapped his fingers and Butterfield sauntered down the aisle carrying a silver tray. He handed Robert a fountain pen and crisp sheet of notepaper bearing the Teabagging family crest.

'Okay,' said Blandon. 'Let's see what we got here.'

He copied the letters fastidiously in reverse, making sure they were all in the right order.

He gazed down at the letters when he'd finished them.

Blandon couldn't believe what he was reading.

This just couldn't be right.

It simply couldn't.

Blandon lifted up the paper and Teabagging gasped.

The words on the papyrus scroll read, 'Vatican Secret Archives.'


## Chapter 99

'What on earth have old Dante and Da Vinci got us into now?' asked Teabagging. 'Events have taken a very serious turn.'

*No kidding*, thought Blandon.

Messing around with the police was one thing, but the Catholic Church? Those guys played hardball.

But what choice did they have?

The police would shoot him as soon as look at him now.

It was very simple.

He'd have to follow this dark treasure hunt to its shocking conclusion.

'I don't understand,' said Florence. 'What does "Vatican Secret Archives" mean?'

'The Vatican Secret Archives is one of the deadliest libraries in the world,' said Robert. 'It contains thousands of years of the Catholic Church's darkest secrets and is completely out of bounds to everyone forever. Except for researchers. But they need to apply for an admission card. And they're not allowed in on weekends.'

'That's the most secret place I've ever heard of,' said Florence.

'I wish the scroll had never mentioned it,' said Blandon.

'So do I,' said Teabagging, fixing Blandon with wizardly wisdom. 'But that is not for us to decide. All we have to decide is what to do with the time that is given to us.'

'Okay,' said Blandon. 'Let's head for these secret archives.'

Teabagging snapped his fingers.

'Butterfield!' he shouted. 'Fire up the Falcon.'


## Chapter 100

Dawn was breaking as Blandon stepped outside into the Piazza Santa Croce. Dr Kakuro's feet were still sticking out of the pit in the ground. The magic square he'd traced on the floor in blood had now gone brown and crusty.

*They really ought to clear that up*, thought Blandon.

Teabagging hobbled across the square and pointed to a sleek white Hawker 731 jet, with twin Garrett TFE-731 engines which each had an inlet diameter of 0.787m, a fan with twenty-two blades and a five-stage compressor with four axial stages and one radial stage.

'What the hell?' gasped Blandon.

'Well, you can hardly expect me to travel with the common man on the omnibus, can you?' chortled Teabagging.

Teabagging led them up the steps to the aircraft's cabin.

Blandon gasped all over again as he saw the interior.

Plush, fully adjustable walnut leather chairs looked out over a spacious cabin featuring flatscreen monitors, a matching leather divan and a four-poster bed. In the middle of the floor, a bubbling Jacuzzi contained three bronzed young men wearing skimpy swimming trunks and sipping Louis Roederer Cristal Champagne from flutes on which the Teabagging coat of arms was engraved.

Teabagging clapped his hands.

'Matthew! Rupert! Benjamin!' he shouted. 'Stop lazing around in that thing and prepare our guests some victuals.'

Butterfield opened the cockpit door. He was now wearing an aviation headset.

'Aircraft prepared for take off, sir,' he said.

'Well, what are you waiting for, man?' yapped Teabagging. 'Get on with it.'

## Chapter 101

Fascist was sitting at his desk at Florence police station and getting ready to fill out his report.

He hated the way his pen-pushing superiors always made him do this. So what if he'd blown up some tedious old duffer's birthplace? He'd rid the world of Robert Blandon, hadn't he?

They ought to give him a medal, not make him fill in a form.

The door swung open and a young officer barged in.

'I'm doing my blasted paperwork,' snarled Fascist. 'This better be important.'

'It is, sir,' said the officer. 'We've had reports that a passenger jet illegally took off from one of the city's ancient squares just a few minutes ago.'

'Ignore it,' said Fascist. 'It's probably just kids having fun.'

'That's not all,' said the officer. 'Eyewitnesses have reported that one of the people who boarded the aircraft was Robert Blandon.'

Fascist jumped up, ripped his report into a thousand tiny pieces and stamped on them.

'Blllllaaaaaannnnnnddddddddoooooonnnnn!' he cried, loud enough to make his desk rattle.

He dashed up ten flights of stairs to the roof of the station and leapt into one of the force's Lockheed AC-130 gunships. He stuck his key in the ignition and pulled away, thundering skyward with incredible speed.

*I'm coming for you, Blandon*, he thought as the ancient Tuscan city dropped away from him.

## Chapter 102

'No thanks,' said Blandon, covering the top of his wine glass as the semi-nude young man offered him a top-up. The five-course meal and bottle of 1945 Romanée-Conti had been exquisite, but he didn't want to overdo it.

He'd need all his wits about him when they got to Vatican City.

Blandon looked out of the window as the engines thundered him southwards, away from Tuscany and towards Lazio. The land below him was brightening as the sun rose.

'So,' said Teabagging. 'Seeing as though our quests have converged, I wonder if you'd care to speculate who's really behind this little charade. The Masons? The Rosicrucians? The Illuminati? The Priory? The Templars?'

'You want the truth?' asked Robert. 'I think it might be all of them at once.'

Teabagging spluttered wine all over his tray in surprise and wiped his mouth with a silk handkerchief.

'You just made me spit approximately five thousand pounds' worth of wine out of my mouth,' said Teabagging. 'I'd hate for it to have been wasted in vain. Are you serious?'

'Of course I'm serious,' said Robert. 'Deadly serious.'

Teabagging's eyes widened.

'Tonight we saw a video which clearly showed the world's most powerful people taking part in a ritual combining the traditions of all those societies,' said Robert. 'Turns out it was filmed inside the giant owl at Bohemian Grove.'

Teabagging's eyes widened even further.

'A good kid who helped us out earlier tonight said something that stuck with me,' continued Blandon. '*The grand unified theory of puzzles*. I think he might have been on to something. What if all those secret societies are really run by the same people? What if one elite group is behind all the secrets our profession has been trying to reveal to the world over the centuries? What if Professor Companion got too close to the truth about who they really are?'

Teabagging's eyes widened even further, but this hurt him so he had to narrow them slightly again.

'Whoever laid your trail must have been privy to the same secret,' said Robert. 'They obviously meant to attract someone who had the knowledge and means to follow a series of obscure clues in locations around the world that are of particular interest to puzzleologists. Someone who would fully understand the shocking revelations waiting at the end of the trail.'

Teabagging gulped.

'Well, we'll find out soon enough, dear boy,' he said.

The jet lurched violently to the right, sending champagne glasses and silver trays crashing to the ground, and sloshing water out of the Jacuzzi.

'What on earth are you playing at, Butterfield?' demanded Teabagging. 'You haven't been imbibing the champagne too, have you?'

'No, sir!' shouted Butterfield from the cockpit. 'Enemy aircraft on our tail!'

## Chapter 103

Blandon glanced out of the window and saw the Lockheed AC-130 on their tail. It had a row of blue flashing lights on top, Florence Police Department decals down the side and a blaring siren.

The gunship banked into a circular turn and fired at them with M61 Vulcan cannons.

Butterfield swerved to the side, dodging the bullets.

'It's me he wants,' said Robert. 'There's no need to put your jet at risk. Find somewhere to land and I'll surrender to him.'

'Not a word of it,' said Teabagging. 'Our quest is far too important to let that little bully stop us.'

Teabagging leant into the aisle and shouted at Butterfield. 'Take her low over St Peter's Square.'

'Would sir like me to perform a crash landing?' asked Butterfield.

'No time for that,' said Teabagging. 'Just take us low

enough to jump out and get back in the sky so the boys can give that idiot hell.'

Teabagging pressed a button on the side of the cabin and a round gun turret rose up on the back of the aircraft. Matthew, Rupert and Benjamin raced over to it and began to fire at Fascist's plane with machine guns.

Teabagging reached under his seat and brought out three folded squares of fabric. He handed two of them to Robert and Florence.

'A parachute?' queried Florence.

'Heavens, no,' said Teabagging. 'Never bother with the things myself. These are windshield tarps. Just pop your hands through the loops at the side and you'll be tickety-boo.'

Blandon unfolded the meagre concave rectangle. It was four yards by two (3.66 metres by 1.83 metres). Robert did the math and worked out it would just about slow his body down enough to survive the fall. But he wished the eccentric old cove had bothered to stock up on parachutes.

At least it explained Teabagging's leg braces.

Robert's stomach churned as the jet lurched lower and lower.

*Here goes nothing*, he thought.


## Chapter 104

Blandon was falling rapidly towards the ground.

*Plummeting.*

He was crashing to earth in a dead drop.

He clutched the loops on either side of the tarp with whitening fingers. The harsh concrete of the ground beneath rose up to meet him at unbelievable speed.

There was no drag on the tarp.

Five hundred feet.

The thing wasn't slowing down at all.

Three hundred feet.

Blandon wondered if he'd done the math wrong.

Two hundred feet.

One hundred feet.

Fifty feet.

He was showing no sign of slowing down as the ground came ever nearer.

Twenty-five feet.

Right at the last minute the drag on the tarpaulin slowed him and he landed safely.

'Phew,' said Blandon. 'That was close.'

A few yards away, Florence and Teabagging were getting up and wiping dirt from their sleeves.

'Told you it would be fine,' said Teabagging. 'So, should we get on with it?'

Blandon stood up and looked around.

He was in St Peter's Square, Vatican City. In the sky above them, Fascist and Teabagging's crew were starting a noisy aerial battle.

## Chapter 105

St Peter's Square is a huge granite plaza in the middle of Vatican City, the papal enclave surrounded by Rome.

Blandon's puzzleology work had brought him here many times. He could scarcely imagine a more apt place for his quest to culminate.

Seen from above, the stones of the square clearly traced

out the shapes of a Templar cross, a Rosicrucian cross with a circumpunct instead of a rose, and a slightly squashed all-seeing eye. And you could probably get a square and compass out of them too.

All the deadliest secret societies were here at the world's holiest square, hiding in plain sight. The truth had been staring everyone in the face all along, but they'd missed it because they hadn't been squinting at an aerial view and imagining shapes on top of it.

Blandon's heart winced as he remembered the time he'd kissed Rome Sidekick in this ancient square after saving the world from a nuclear bomb the Illuminati had planted inside Pope John Paul II. He wondered if Rome Sidekick was okay, and if he should text her later on if Florence turned him down.

There wasn't time to think about that now.

*They had work to do.*

Teabagging began to run towards St Peter's Basilica.

'Where are you going?' shouted Blandon.

'To the secret archives,' said Teabagging. 'You have to enter them by a door hidden behind St Peter's Throne.'

Blandon chuckled to himself. This was actually a myth invented by the Catholic Church to stop the public discovering the true location of the archives, up the hill from the Santa Ana Gate.

Blandon himself had been inside the real archives many times. In fact, he'd last been there just three months ago, researching his theory that an ancient volume of wordsearches had been removed from the Bible by the Emperor Constantine at the First Council of Nicaea.

'The real archives are this way,' said Blandon, pointing to the north of the plaza.

Teabagging gasped and ran quickly back to Blandon, his

legs straining eagerly at their metal braces.

Blandon led them purposefully towards the archives. He checked his watch. It was just coming up to half past eight. Opening time.

They turned into the brick pathway leading to the entrance of the archive building. Inside, a small bespectacled woman was perched neatly behind a desk.

'What is the purpose of your visit?' she asked.

'Research,' replied Blandon.

'I see,' she said. 'And do you have a visitor's pass?'

Blandon's heart raced. He'd been issued with a pass last time he was here, but he had no idea if it would still be in his wallet. He'd taken a few receipts out when he was doing his expenses a couple of weeks ago.

Was it possible the pass could have fallen out then?

*No, it was there.* Right next to his Royal Society of Puzzleologists membership card.

He took out the visitor's pass and showed it to the woman.

'Very well,' she said, waving them on.

Blandon, Teabagging and Florence walked down a long hallway to a set of wide oak doors.

'This is so secret,' said Florence. 'This is probably the most secret place I've ever been.'

Behind her, Teabagging was dabbing hot tears from his eyes. 'To think that I'm about to see inside the world's most exclusive archive. It simply beggars belief.'

## Chapter 106

Blandon threw open the doors to reveal a large, dark and silent room. Freestanding glass cubicles lined the huge space, airtight structures protecting the ancient texts from humidity.

'I can't believe I'm really here,' said Teabagging, salty tears running down his cheeks. 'Wait until I tell the fellows at the Royal Puzzleology Institute about this.'

'Careful with those tears,' said Blandon. 'Anything that adds to the humidity of the room can help to damage these precious artefacts.'

Teabagging stopped crying.

'So here we are,' said Florence. 'The end of the trail. But what are we meant to be looking out for? There are a lot of things here.'

'No kidding,' said Blandon. 'There are 52 miles (84km) of shelves in here, amounting to more than 35,000 volumes in the selective archive alone. Even I haven't read them all.'

Teabagging wandered over to a nearby table and began to flip through ancient parchments.

'This is explosive,' he whispered to himself. 'This changes everything.'

He was looking at classified documents proving the Vatican's involvement in the fake moon landings. He picked up a Polaroid of Pope Paul VI and Buzz Aldrin enjoying a joke on the lunar set.

Blandon chuckled to himself. Teabagging was like a kid in a candy store. He'd been no different the first time he'd come to this place. But it wasn't what they'd come here for today.

'There'll be time for that later,' said Blandon.

'Sorry, darling,' said Teabagging, trying to peel his eyes away from the outrageous evidence.

'Look at this,' said Florence.

She was standing by one of the glass cubicles. Inside, the end of one of the shelves had been covered with hundreds of symbols.

The Templar cross.

The Rosicrucian cross.

The square and compass.

The all-seeing eye.

Blandon and Teabagging rushed over to the cubicle.

'The symbols we've been following since Florence,' said Blandon.

'And the symbols I've been following since Egypt,' said Teabagging.

'Well, it looks like we've come to our final destination,' said Florence.

Blandon gulped.

Our final destination.

*No kidding.*

It was well known that these cubicles were starved of oxygen. The official line was that the oxygen would damage the sacred texts, although Blandon suspected it was to impair the brainpower of researchers so they wouldn't be able to think straight and work out the Catholic Church's role in the New Coke scandal of 1985.

But they had to go in. They'd come too far to simply turn around, walk out, take a few photos at the Trevi Fountain and the Spanish Steps and discover a surprisingly inexpensive little place off the tourist trail that does a delightful risotto and has a terrific wine list.

'A word of warning,' said Blandon. 'I've been in these

places before and it can be very hard to breathe. It's like a vacuum in there. I'm not sure what we're going to find, but we need to get out as soon as possible.'

He stepped over to the electronic revolving door on the side of the cubicle and pressed the button next to it.

The door shuddered forward and Blandon leapt into the gap.

He tried not to imagine he was falling into an abandoned well as he stepped into the glass vault. His ears, nose and eyes popped and he felt a horrible dryness in his mouth.

Teabagging and Florence followed him in. Blandon watched their pulmonary capillaries dilate.

'I feel... like... I'm scuba... diving,' said Florence.

'And I feel... like I'm... in the sauna... at my private... members' club,' said Teabagging.

'Okay,' said Blandon. 'Let's examine the shelves before our air runs out.'

He dashed down to the far end of the five rows of shelves. He cocked his head to the side and read the gold-leaf lettering on the spines of the leather-bound volumes.

*How the Catholic Church Cancelled the Original Series of* Star Trek.

*Why the Catholic Church Made the Microsoft Zune Fail.*

*The Fashion Predictions of Nostradamus.*

*Fascinating tomes,* thought Blandon.

But he didn't have time to read them right now.

He was searching for... *what?*

'Over here,' shouted Florence, who'd been examining the shelves nearest the door.

Blandon and Teabagging ran to her.

Florence was pointing at a large volume that had no words on the spine, but instead featured a Templar cross,

Rosicrucian cross, all-seeing eye and square and compass embossed in gold leaf.

'This must be the fellow we're after,' said Teabagging.

Florence grabbed the spine, pulled the book out and opened it up.

Blandon, Florence and Teabagging all gasped when they saw what was inside.


## Chapter 107

'Blank,' said Florence. 'The pages are all blank.'

'The book was nothing more than bait,' yelled Blandon, his heart thumping. 'This is a trap.'

Blandon dashed over to the revolving door and slammed his hand on the button next to it. Nothing happened.

He tried again.

Still nothing.

The connection was as dead as he'd soon be due to the lack of oxygen in the room.

He pushed his weight against the door, but it didn't budge.

Blandon told his heart not to speed up, as this would only make him snort away the precious oxygen sooner. The contrary muscle ignored him, beating its terrified rhythm faster and faster.

'We need to get out,' yelled Blandon. 'Before the air runs out.'

Teabagging ripped off one of his leg braces and bashed it against the glass. It bounced off without leaving a crack.

'It's no use, dear boy,' he said. 'This is reinforced glass.'

An eerie calm began to sweep through Blandon's mind. He ignored it, knowing it was the final stage before death.

'Let's see if it can withstand this,' shouted Florence. She flung herself against one of the shelves, trying to tip it onto the glass.

'Must we?' asked Teabagging. 'Think about the precious documents that might be damaged.'

'I'm afraid it's our only option,' said Blandon. 'It's us or the documents.'

Teabagging sighed and joined Florence and Blandon behind the shelf. They took shallow breaths and shoved it forward with their remaining strength.

The shelf toppled forward and slammed against the glass.

The glass withstood this new attack with an ease that would have made other pieces of glass jealous.

Blandon stared at it in desperation. He couldn't believe it. They'd come all this way, only to die without even finding out what it was all about.

Blandon lowered himself to the carpeted floor. The lack of oxygen was making him hallucinate bright purple symbols in his field of vision. He was about to explain the ancient secret meanings of them when he remembered that he was the only one who could see them.

'Look,' shouted Florence.

Blandon forced his weak head to turn to the puzzleology graduate. She was pointing at the bottom of the shelf.

A small gap in the floor could be seen where the shelf had been perched. Blandon crawled over to it and looked inside. As his eyes adjusted to the gloom, he could see a narrow space below.

*A secret passageway.*

## Chapter 108

The Pathfinder watched the three tiny figures crawl down into the space beneath the bookshelf on his CCTV screen.

Blandon had done well.

Better than he'd expected.

He'd assumed his apprentice would end his little game back in the Casa di Dante. Unfortunately that ridiculous police inspector had chosen to mess things up.

It didn't matter.

It only meant that Blandon's path had crossed with that other little fly in his ointment, Sir Lee Teabagging.

And now he'd have the pleasure of killing them both at once.

The Pathfinder loaded his Heckler and Koch Mark 23 and made his way to the final destination.

## Chapter 109

Blandon led Florence and Teabagging towards the end of the ancient tunnel. He'd heard all about these *passettos*, the slender passages that ran underneath Vatican City and were used to carry Popes to safety in times of crisis. But he'd had no idea one of them linked the Vatican Secret Archives to...

*Where?*

Blandon didn't know.

But wherever he was headed, it had to be better than the airless glass cubicle they'd escaped from.

*Didn't it?*

The tunnel came to an abrupt stop ahead of them. Metal

rungs lined the wall, leading to a square wooden door with rusty hinges.

He began to climb.

## Chapter 110

Blandon threw the door aside, his head still spinning from lack of air. As his lungs drank in the sweet oxygen his eyes drank in the scene above him and his brain spewed confusion.

*Am I in heaven?* thought Blandon.

Directly above him, he could see God, dressed in a swirling white cloak, reaching out and giving the spark of life to a buff naked man.

Blandon climbed out of the tunnel and looked around.

*No, he wasn't in heaven.*

As reason flooded back to Blandon's impressive mind, he realized he was actually in the Sistine Chapel.

Famous for its lavish decoration, the Sistine Chapel is frescoed throughout by renowned artists such as Michelangelo, Botticelli and Pinturicchio.

As he'd climbed from the tunnel, Blandon had been looking at *The Creation of Adam*, the most famous part of Michelangelo's ceiling. It's that one where their fingers are almost touching.

Florence and Teabagging climbed out.

'The Sistine Chapel,' said Teabagging. 'What can it all possibly mean?'

'I don't know,' said Florence. 'But I think we're about to find out.'

She pointed to the corner of the chapel, where a dark

figure was striding towards them.

'I'm so glad we finally get to meet,' said the figure.

He was wearing a thick black monk's cowl with a white all-seeing eye embossed on the front. His face was covered with a Knight's Templar helmet with a masonic blindfold stretched around it. In his hand he was carrying a Heckler and Koch Mark 23.

'And after we find out he's going to kill us,' said Florence.

## Chapter 111

'Who are you?' asked Blandon. 'Why have you brought us here?'

'I am the Pathfinder,' said the figure. 'I'm the head of the Rosicrucilluminatemplarmasons, also known as the Conspiratorium. Also known as the Order from Chaos.'

*Ordo ab chao.*

Blandon swallowed his confusion.

He remembered what Giuseppe had said.

*The grand unified theory of puzzles.*

But what was it all for?

'What do your group want?' asked Blandon. 'World domination?'

The figure cackled. 'Oh, nothing as boring as that, I can assure you.'

'Well, would you mind telling us who the bloody hell you are?' asked Teabagging. 'I've spent a lot of money following your trail. The least you can do is furnish me with an explanation.'

'It would really be a lot kinder of me to just shoot you

without telling you,' said the man.

'Kinder?' spluttered Teabagging. 'How could killing us in a desperate state of ignorance possibly be kinder?'

'Trust me,' said the man. 'It would.'

'Please tell us,' pleaded Florence. 'We've been through such a lot to get here.'

The man sighed. 'I suppose I owe you an explanation, at least. But you won't like it.'

He untied his thick black cowl and let it fall to the floor. Underneath, he was wearing a tweed jacket, black turtleneck sweater, khaki pants and loafers.

'A puzzleologist?' muttered Blandon in shock. 'But who?'

The figure lifted up his blindfolded helmet and let it clang to the floor.

Blandon, Florence and Teabagging let out a loud gasp.

'Professor Companion?' asked Blandon.

'Father?' asked Florence.


## Chapter 112

'Yes, my child, it is I,' began Professor Companion. 'I'm sorry I had to pretend I'd been murdered and then pulled open my stomach, scrawled riddles in blood and arranged my entrails into visual clues. It was the only way.'

'Was Fascist in on it too?' asked Blandon. 'Someone must have let you out the morgue.'

'That idiot knew nothing about it,' said Professor Companion. 'He never gets round to taking bodies down to the morgue for ages. I was counting on his incompetence, and he didn't let me down.'

'What about the rest of your department?' asked Blandon. 'Were they just pretending to be dead?'

'No, I'm afraid they had to go,' said Professor Companion. 'They were getting too close to the truth. Asking too many awkward questions.'

'What truth?' asked Blandon. 'That this Conspiratorium of yours is secretly running the world?'

'Of course not,' said Professor Companion. 'Don't you get it? They were beginning to work out the *real* truth. That *no one* is secretly running the world.'

Blandon's mind spun with confusion.

*No one was secretly running the world?*

The old man was just rambling now. His words made no sense.

'My staff were starting to wonder if sinister secret societies really exist. And if all conspiracy theories, alternate histories and new age pseudosciences are just comforting stories that people tell themselves to hide from the fact that the world is completely random. Stuff just happens.

'Every day the difficult questions were coming,' Companion continued. 'Isn't it more likely that we actually landed on the moon than that thousands of people agreed to perpetrate a hoax and keep it secret for the rest of their lives? Isn't it incredibly likely that Lee Harvey Oswald really did kill JFK? Why isn't there any evidence whatsoever for all this stuff about the Priory of Sion hushing up the bloodline of Christ? And isn't all this stuff about the Illuminati and Freemasons running the world clearly bullshit of the highest order?

'I could see they were getting too close to the truth. And I knew I had to stop them.'

Blandon snorted with derision. 'If these theories are just comforting myths, why are you so keen to keep the so-called truth about them secret?'

'It's precisely because these myths are comforting that my organization is dedicated to protecting them,' said Professor Companion. 'The Conspiratorium was established by Dante Alighieri in 1320. He noticed that whenever something bad happened, one of his friends would always blame the Knights Templar, who he thought were secretly controlling the world. At first this annoyed Dante, but he soon saw how much hope these unfounded beliefs gave to his friend.

'Dante knew that the world would need the Conspiratorium one day. He knew that there would come a time when traditional beliefs would fade and people would need new myths. Since then, we've done everything we can to convince the world that defunct groups like the Illuminati and the Knights Templar live on, that hoaxes like the Priory of Sion and the Rosicrucians are genuine and that innocuous groups of old men like the Freemasons are sinister goat-humpers.

'Whenever I see a packed theatre crowd listening to some nutjob going on about how the British royal family are lizards, or I hear an irate caller to a US talk show claiming that the US government launches terrorist attacks on itself, or I pass a queue of fans outside a bookshop desperate to be the first to get their hands on a new conspiracy thriller, I know our work is not in vain.

'Those people have belief. They have a reason to live.'

Blandon shook his head with pity. The man had clearly gone mad.

Florence wiped a tear from her eye. 'Oh papa! I don't care why you had to kill them all! I'm just glad you're alive.'

Professor Companion swung round, pointing his Heckler and Koch Mark 23 at his daughter.

'I'm sorry, my flower,' he said. 'But I cannot let you live with this knowledge. I swore an oath to the Conspiratorium that overrides all personal ties. I wish you'd never got involved with this ridiculous mullet-headed American and this disabled but surprisingly mobile English aristocrat. My treasure hunt of doom was intended only for them.'

'Why was it intended for me, anyway?' asked Blandon. 'What did I have to do with your staff?'

'You were the only person they still respected,' said Professor Companion. 'Even as the mundane truth about the world was suggesting itself to them, their love for you remained strong. They gladly risked their lives to help the world's greatest puzzleology icon, and became sitting ducks for my assassin.

'Later today the world will wake up to the news that world's greatest puzzleologist, the field's most powerful patron, and the entire puzzleology department of the University of Florence have all been killed in mysterious circumstances. Just as the message boards are lighting up, I'll release the faked footage my colleague showed you in the Casa di Dante, confirming the existence of a goat-humping secret sect made up of the most powerful people in the world.

'Sceptics will be converted, believers will see their deepest fears confirmed. More people will believe fanciful, convoluted notions than ever before, and the noble work of the Conspiratorium will be done.'

Professor Companion pointed his gun at Teabagging.

'So, I hope I've satisfied your desire to know the truth,' said Professor Companion. 'It can't be pleasant to find out everything you've ever believed is drivel just before you die, but I gave you the option of ignorant bliss.'

Professor Companion lifted up the gun and pulled the trigger.

### Chapter 113

Boom.

### Chapter 114

No, really. Boom.

### Chapter 115

The bullet came flying out of Professor Companion's pistol at exactly the same time as what sounded like a deafening clap of thunder crashed above them.

Blandon glanced over to see Teabagging leap aside and then up just in time to see a crack of white light appear from the end of God's finger.

Blandon grabbed Florence and shoved her out of the way as the heavy chunk of ceiling with God painted on it crashed down towards the floor.

It landed right on top of Professor Companion, splatting him like a rotten fruit. Blood drenched the elaborate floor of the renowned chapel.

'Well, I don't think he's faking it this time,' chuckled Blandon as Professor Companion's decapitated head rolled past them.

Another huge section of ceiling, this time the bit with Adam on it, crashed down to the floor.

Something emerged through the hole in the roof. It was the nose of Fascist's Lockheed AC-130 gunship. The aircraft had precariously come to rest on what remained of the roof.

'Bllaanndddooonnn!' came a familiar voice from above them.

Fascist jumped out of his plane, plummeted down through the gap in the ceiling, landed on his feet and stalked towards Blandon, who could do nothing but cower helplessly on the floor.

'Finally, I get to complete my work,' snarled Fascist, taking his gun out of his holster and pointing it at the frightened Harvard puzzleologist.

Fascist stopped in front of Blandon and placed his finger on the trigger.

Blandon flinched, steeling himself for the searing pain of the bullet.

It never came.

*Thud.*

Fascist was swept to the floor by a thick metal crosier.

'What the hell?' asked Blandon.

Standing behind the felled police inspector, brandishing the crosier, was Pope Francis.

'Not on my patch,' snarled Pope Francis.

## Chapter 116

Robert grasped Florence's hand and stared down from the roof of St Peter's Basilica. The square beneath was filled with TV crews frantically trying to piece together the morning's events.

No one seemed to know exactly what had happened.

But they did agree on one thing.

*Robert Blandon was a hero.*

Pope Francis hadn't wanted any of the credit for taking Fascist down, so Blandon had agreed to take it instead.

'Thanks for helping me, buddy,' Robert had said, clasping his hand on the old man's vestment-clad shoulder. 'I'd do the same for you.'

'I know you would,' the Pope had said. 'We don't always see eye to eye, Robert. But you're a good kid. The world could do with a few more like you.'

The Vatican press office had released a statement detailing how Robert Blandon had single-handedly thwarted an attacker who'd crashed his plane into the Sistine Chapel and was bent on destroying the ancient art treasures of the church.

Puzzleology enthusiasts had gathered in squares and plazas around the world, chanting Blandon's name and holding placards of his image.

*Great*, Blandon had thought wryly. *More fans.*

While all the frenzy of confusion had been going on in the square below, Florence had taken Robert up to the roof and made passionate love to him as a reward for saving her life.

'What the hell?' Blandon had asked as Florence pushed him to the floor and greedily straddled him, her eyes burning with mischievous and unconventional flames as she'd consumed him.

Now they were looking down at the square and reflecting on their adventure.

'I can't believe it was just twenty-four hours ago that I touched down in Florence,' said Blandon. 'It seems like a lifetime ago.'

'At least you got some sleep when you were in hospital with that serious head wound,' said Florence. 'I've been awake since yesterday morning. And I've lost my father twice in that time.'

Blandon grasped Florence's hand tighter and gazed into her eyes. 'I hate to say it, Florence, but you lost your father a long time ago.'

'I know,' said Florence. 'I can't believe he was saying all that stuff about secret societies not existing and conspiracy theories being comforting fantasies. If that were true, everyone in our profession would have totally wasted their lives.'

A tear was running down Florence's cheek. Blandon cradled her to his chest.

'Try not to remember him that way,' said Blandon. 'He'd obviously lost his mind. My best guess is that the Illuminati used the fluoride in his water supply to control his thoughts. It happens a lot.'

'And all those dead puzzleologists,' said Florence. 'What will everyone think?'

'They'll probably never find out,' said Blandon. 'The Florence police department will have enough on their plate explaining why one of their inspectors went rogue. They'll probably blame their deaths on a gas leak in the department.'

'And will you back them up?' asked Florence.

'I guess so,' said Blandon.

But won't that make you part of a conspiracy?' asked Florence. 'The kind of thing you've dedicated your life to uncovering?'

'Maybe,' said Blandon. 'But a good conspiracy. Not a bad conspiracy like the ones the Illuminati or the US government do.'

'I see,' said Florence. 'Sometimes this whole puzzleology game is so confusing.'

Blandon grabbed Florence's chin and probed her with romantic eyes.

'Chin up, kid,' he said. 'You're a good puzzleologist. You might even become a great one.'

'I'll never be as good as you, Robert,' said Florence.

'I know,' said Blandon. 'But I still think you've got a hell of a lot of puzzling in you. That's why I called the Chancellor of Florence University earlier on and told him to make you the new head of the puzzleology faculty.'

Hope and wonder exploded in Florence's eyes.

'The new head of the puzzleology faculty?' she breathed. 'Do you think I'm ready for it?'

'Sure, why not?' asked Robert. 'After all, I think they've got a couple of vacancies.'

Florence and Robert laughed long and hard as they thought about all the dead bodies they'd seen.

## Chapter 117

'Mr Blandon,' shouted a voice. 'If you could spare a moment.'

*Great*, thought Blandon. *I've been spotted.*

But when he turned to look, he saw not a rabid fan, but a cardinal wearing a black cassock, red sash and scarlet zucchetto.

'It won't take long,' said the cardinal. 'Just a little something we'd like you to see.'

The cardinal led Blandon and Florence down a stone stairwell and along a lavish corridor to an ornate door. He flung it aside and led them back into the Sistine Chapel.

*These guys work fast*, thought Blandon.

Just a few hours ago, the floor had been covered in rubble from the collapsed ceiling and blood from the squashed professor. Now its patterned marble floors were spotless.

'Well done,' said Blandon. 'You guys really pulled out the stops.'

'It is not the floor we wanted to show you,' said the cardinal. 'It is the ceiling.'

Robert Blandon looked up.

'What the hell?' he spluttered.

'Maybe you should be asking "What the heaven?"' grinned the cardinal.

The ceiling of the chapel had now been completely restored. The cardinals had restored the *Creation of Adam* as best as they could, too. But the section of the fresco that depicted God had been irreparably damaged in the accident, so they'd replaced it with a new one.

In the place where the elderly, white-bearded man with the swirling white robe had been, there was now a younger man wearing a tweed jacket, black turtleneck, khaki trousers and loafers.

The fresco no longer showed God giving the spark of life to Adam. It showed Robert Blandon doing it.

Blandon winced.

His colleagues back in Harvard weren't going to let him hear the last of this. But he knew the gesture had been a sincere one.

'Thanks,' said Blandon. 'You did good.'

## Chapter 118

'Care to join us, Robert?' shouted Teabagging from the Jacuzzi he was sharing with his three young helpers.

'I think I'll sit it out,' said Blandon.

Blandon stared out the cabin window at the shimmering Atlantic Ocean and sipped his Krug Brut Vintage 1988. Teabagging and his crew had kindly agreed to give him a lift back to Harvard after they'd dropped Florence back at her university.

*Florence Companion*, thought Blandon, her name floating sweetly through his mind like blossom on the summer breeze. He wondered if he should have given her his real number.

*Never mind*, he thought. *There'll be another generic attractive female companion along soon.*

'Looks like our friend Purgatorio will be going away for quite some time,' said Teabagging.

He pointed out the large flatscreen monitor embedded in the wall of the cabin. A news report showed Fascist being bundled into the back of a police car. A caption reading 'Florence police inspector accused of trying to assassinate Robert Blandon' flashed up on screen as a crowd of angry puzzleology fans surrounded the police car.

'It's your boys they should really be cheering,' said Blandon. 'If they hadn't forced Fascist's plane down onto the Sistine Chapel, Professor Companion would have killed us all.'

'My boys did a wondrous job as usual,' said Teabagging, clasping the thighs of two of his muscly assistants. 'But your struggle for the truth in the face of danger has been an inspiration to thousands around the world.'

He pointed to the screen.

The report showed grateful crowds holding up Blandon placards in New York's Times Square.

It cut to a giant bronze Blandon statue being erected in Moscow's Red Square.

It cut to an overjoyed woman in Delhi holding up a baby which was wearing a tiny tweed jacket, black turtleneck and khaki pants.

Finally, they showed a jubilant crowd at Beijing's Tiananmen Gate ripping down a portrait of Chairman Mao and replacing it with one of Blandon.

'You've really hit the big time now, old boy,' said Teabagging, his eyebrows dancing playfully.

'Tell me about it,' sighed Blandon. 'As if my classes weren't crowded enough.'

Blandon imagined what the scrum to get inside next semester's puzzleology lectures was going to look like. They'd need to double the Harvard door security staff.

'It's just as well,' said Teabagging. 'We'll need all the

help we can get if we're going to get rid of the rest of the Conspiratorium.'

Blandon spluttered champagne down his turtleneck.

'You think there are more of them?' he asked, exasperated.

'Of course,' said Teabagging. 'You don't think that old professor could have led me on a merry dance around Africa, America and Europe on his own, do you? His organization probably has hundreds of members around the world.'

Blandon's mind boggled.

Hundreds of people who believed that conspiracy theories and alternate histories were nothing but the crazed ranting of paranoid fools.

*What was the world coming to?*

Blandon settled back in his seat and sipped his champagne. He'd had a busy couple of days but he was finally going to get some peace and quiet.

## Epilogue

The tattooed man pulled his BMW S1000RR bike to a stop outside Harvard airport and ran up to the arrivals entrance just as the sleek white Hawker 731 jet was touching down.

Blandon had enjoyed a lucky escape inside the Sistine Chapel. But his luck was about to run out.

He took his 9mm Glock 17 Gen 4 out of his pocket and waited.

*To kill him.*